By IAN I. MITROFF
(as author, coauthor)

THE SUBJECTIVE SIDE OF SCIENCE:
A PHILOSOPHICAL INQUIRY INTO
THE PSYCHOLOGY OF THE APOLLO MOON SCIENTISTS

METHODOLOGICAL APPROACHES TO SOCIAL SCIENCES

CHALLENGING STRATEGIC PLANNING ASSUMPTIONS:
THEORY, CASES, AND TECHNIQUES

CREATING A DIALECTICAL SOCIAL SCIENCE:
CONCEPTS, METHODS, AND MODELS

THE 1980 CENSUS: POLICYMAKING AMID TURBULENCE

Stakeholders
of the
Organizational Mind

*Toward a New View
of Organizational
Policy Making*

Ian I. Mitroff

Foreword by Richard O. Mason

Stakeholders
of the
Organizational Mind

Jossey-Bass Publishers
San Francisco • Washington • London • 1983

STAKEHOLDERS OF THE ORGANIZATIONAL MIND
Toward a New View of Organizational Policy Making
by Ian I. Mitroff

Library of Congress Cataloging in Publication Data

Mitroff, Ian I.
      Stakeholders of the organizational mind.

      Bibliography: p. 165
      Includes index.
      1. Organizational behavior. 2. Management—
Psychological aspects. I. Title.
HD58.7.M57   1983   658.4'01'9   83-48161
ISBN 0-87589-580-8

Manufactured in the United States of America

The paper in this book meets the guidelines for
permanence and durability of the Committee on
Production Guidelines for Book Longevity of the
Council on Library Resources.

JACKET DESIGN BY WILLI BAUM

FIRST EDITION

Code 8327

A joint publication in
The Jossey-Bass Management Series
and
The Jossey-Bass Social and Behavioral Science Series

Consulting Editors
Organizations and Their Management

Warren Bennis
University of Southern California

Richard O. Mason
University of Arizona

Ian I. Mitroff
University of Southern California

Foreword

Bashō, the pilgrim poet, ventured into Japan's most remote regions with his friend, Sora. As they traveled, they would pause occasionally, whenever the beauty of the moment captured them, to savor and revere their surroundings. Bashō then recorded their thoughts in lovely prose sprinkled with short poems known as haiku. He entitled the resulting book *The Narrow Road to a Far Province.*

For the over eighteen years I have known Ian Mitroff, he too has been on such a journey. He has been on a journey into the remote recesses of the mind. And I, from time to time, have been his Sora, sharing in the excitement of his discoveries, recording them with him so that others might glimpse places he had been.

This book is a travelogue describing the current findings from Mitroff's never-ending journey. It relates his theory of mind as he has been able to formulate it thus far. Managers and theoreticians alike will benefit by following Mitroff's journey.

A practicing manager can see the relevance of *Stakeholders of the Organizational Mind* if he or she will only reflect for a moment on a strategy that went awry. Recall, as an illustration, that during the 1950s, Addressograph-Multigraph dominated the addressing machines market with their automatic imprinting system, which used embossed metal plates. As data processing technology improved and became more accessible to a broader clientele, computer printed labels emerged as a highly competitive substitute for the traditional addressograph machine. Yet, the company proceeded with its "don't-tamper-with-success" philosophy until 1968, when it reacted with a four-year flurry of new product releases. By then, it was too late. Fifteen of the twenty-one releases were flops. Finally, in 1975, Roy L. Ash was brought in from the outside to try to turn things around.

How can this happen to managers and the companies they guide? Mitroff has an answer. Beginning in Chapter Six and continuing in subsequent chapters, he describes the archetypes that lie deep within our minds and guide our most basic life decisions. One such archetype is the Absolutely Perfect Circle, which signifies wholeness, completeness, and perfection. It becomes, as Jung pointed out, a god image. Could it be that executives at Addressograph were living out this archetype? Or, to use another illustration, is it possible that the executives for Britain's White Star Line truly believed that the Titanic was unsinkable?

There is, of course, a plethora of other archetypes that may inhabit our minds, including "great mother," "evil mother," wizard, hermit, chessplayer, and chiliast. In our roles as managers, Mitroff helps us to think about how these archetypes function as fundamental assumptions underlying our decisions. While his model is primarily intended for managers and professionals at work, it also provides valuable insights for social science researchers who study these people. Before we elaborate on Mitroff's theory of the mind, however, it is helpful to see from whence he started.

Throughout his career, Mitroff has worked with managers, scientists, engineers, teachers, and policy makers while they were in the process of conducting their business. They have tended to be white-collar workers, middle- to upper-middle-class people whose work involves knowledge, the flow of information. Not mainstream America, perhaps, but an important and growing segment of the population. Mitroff's theory of the mind is intended primarily to help these practicing professionals to design and manage sociotechnical systems. It is not intended to heal the sick or actualize the superior.

Freud, we know, worked with hysterics—people like Elisabeth von R. and the Wolf Man—many on the verge of total psychological disintegration. So the rather pessimistic view of human beings that emerges from his writings might well reflect this particular experience. Abraham Maslow, however, explicitly selected high-potential, high-achievement people as the objects of his investigations. Thomas Jefferson was his hero and he was intrigued by the "so different from the run-of-the-mill people in the world." Maslow's emphasis on self-actualization then, may also be the result of this selected experience.

Mitroff has worked with people who design and manage things. As Freud sought to eliminate psychological barriers to living a satisfactory life and as Maslow sought to eliminate psychological barriers to realizing one's full potential, Mitroff has sought to eliminate psychological barriers to creating and managing sociotechnical systems. Originally trained as an engineer, Mitroff began with studies of engineers in the process of design. By means of a simulation model, he demonstrated that the social and psychological context the engineer worked in highly influenced his or her design. Technology, thus, was a partial resultant of psychology. But, how did it work?

Pursuing this question, Mitroff did two things. He immersed himself in psychological literature, especially the writings of Carl Gustav Jung and his followers. Furthermore, he sought other arenas in which to test his embryonic theories. The Apollo project presented the appropriate opportunity. Realizing that the moon rocks would represent the very first tangible empirical evidence about the moon, Mitroff set out to study the social and psychological processes by which this evidence would be integrated into prevailing theories. His results were published in a book entitled *The Subjective Side of Science*. In his study, Mitroff found that different types of lunar scientists had different positions on issues. Having received the data, the different types shifted their scientific judgments in different ways and at different rates of speed. Most important, they evolved social systems to handle these scientific problems along with rules of social control that denied some potential researchers access to data. As a result, some promising research avenues were never explored. Why?

Mitroff's studies led him to conclude that Jung's psychological types explained much of the scientists' social and psychological behavior in their professional roles. This conclusion was so compelling that he and Ralph Kilmann went on to generalize it in a book entitled *Methodological Approaches to Social Science*.

Meanwhile, Mitroff turned his attention to another arena: managers in the process of making strategy and policy. During the past eight years or so, Mitroff and I have worked with the U.S. Bureau of Census (see Mitroff, Mason, and Barabba, 1983b), U.S. Forest Service, Department of Education, Department of Energy, representatives of the chemical industry, and a host of private corporations on problems of policy and strategy. In addition, Mitroff has worked with his wife, Donna, in the fields of education and media and with Ralph Kilmann and James Emmoff in private organizations. These engagements have provided him with a breadth of exposure to organizational America.

Because of the real (as opposed to experimental) circumstances in which he has conducted his studies, Mitroff focuses on complexity. He rejects the closed form, soluable "toy" problems he learned as an engineer and turns instead to the "bloomin', blustering confusion" of everyday life, in which problems have many dimensions, many forces are at work, and many different values are in conflict. Furthermore, all these dimensions, forces, and values are interrelated in complicated ways. For example, a manager must deal simultaneously with distant external forces and deep internal personal forces, all reflecting aspects of the past, present, and future. What is perplexing is that there are no known analytical approaches to solving problems of this nature.

As a result, Mitroff's concept of the mind is not mechanical, and thus differs from so many developments in psychology that assume a mechanistic model of mind. John B. Watson studied the maze learning behavior of rats. B. F. Skinner postulated a stimulus-response-reinforcement cycle to include environmentally induced operant behavior. And Edward C. Tolman developed a theory of goal-directed purposive behaviorism. Each of these theories assumes that the mind is a complex network of cause and effect chains. None seeks to understand Koestler's "ghost" in the machine.

Mitroff does. In so doing, he has conceived what may be the broadest—in terms of its time and space dimensions—theory of mind yet proposed. He goes beyond Freud and Jung. In the spirit of Nietzsche, Freud believed that the ego, superego, and id were affected by repressed and sublimated aspects of one's *own* life experience and that the trauma of humanity could be encapsulated in the events of one's own life, for example, in a child's relations with his parents. The "talking cure" was designed to effect release and thus to free up a person's life.

Jung went further: The unconscious did not relate just to one's personal experience but also served as the seat of universal primordial images he called *archetypes*. Jung studied the myths, stories, rites, and ceremonies of an extensive set of cultures and he discovered patterns. These eternal patterns, which Mitroff summarizes in Chapters Six and Seven, were revealed in people's dreams and everyday life experiences.

Jung extended Freud by making mind a product of a past that transcended a single lifetime. In his quest for depth, however, Jung de-emphasized the effect that the broad contemporary social environment also has on the mind. At this point, Mitroff steps in. Mitroff discovered that it is impossible to work with managers and other professionals who are designing social systems without taking into account a great variety of external forces. Government, customers, clients, competitors, suppliers, allies, and a host of other entities all compete for a place in the manager's mind. Furthermore, in the making of strategy, policy, and plans, the crucial elements are the future behavior of these entities together with the assumptions the professional makes about the future behavior of those who affect his or her environment. So Mitroff proposes a concept of mind that deals with the past, present, and future as they are revealed in the mind's external, immediate, and deep internal regions.

I am reminded of the description in Dickens's *A Christmas Carol* of Ebenezer Scrooge, "a grasping old sinner," partner and heir of old Jacob Marley, stockbroker, and employer of Bob Cratchit, his clerk. Scrooge loves no one, is loved by no one. But one Christmas Eve he is visited by three ghosts: *Christmas Past,* who reminds him of the girl whose love he forsook to grow rich; *Christmas Present,* who shows him Bob Cratchit's poor but happy family; and *Christmas Future,* who reveals Scrooge, dead, the prey of Irish harpies and the object of public ridicule. This powerful psychological experience results in Scrooge totally changing his nature and becoming a cheerful, loving, and, as it turns out, loved old man.

Mitroff's model carries many of the tenets implied in Dickens's story. Mitroff argues that managers should search the past, present, and future for active "stakeholders" in their lives and that they should reach as far beyond themselves and as deeply within themselves as possible to find them. Stakeholders are all those entities, parties, actors, organizations, groups, individuals—internal and external to the organization—that affect and are affected by its policies. This quest will lead to real people, groups, and organizations that are influencing factors; it will also lead to Jungian archetypes.

Although Jung's work has had a powerful influence on Mitroff, traces of Gestalt theory and philosophical pragmatism are also to be found in his model. I find Kurt Lewin's *life space* model similar to Mitroff's. A Lewinian life space includes the person, the goals he or she is seeking, the negative states the person is trying to avoid, the barriers that restrict the person's movements, and the paths the person must follow in order to achieve his or her goals. In Mitroff's model these urges or forces would be primarily ego-state stakeholders. Mitroff argues that understanding these is necessary but not sufficient for a full understanding of mind. The mind also encompasses a set of external, distant stakeholders. And there is a set of deep-seated, eternal, archetypical stakeholders. These Mitroff employs in addition to Lewin's life space concept in his model of stakeholders of the mind.

The influence of pragmatist philosophy comes from C. West Churchman and the systems approach tradition he rep-

resents. In systems theory terms, stakeholders are the teleological components of a teleological system. That is, each stakeholder has a will of its own and pursues its own goals as well as
those of the system as a whole. Teleological theory implies that
the mind is composed of a collection of entities, each of which
is both in cooperation *and* in competition with the personality
as a whole. Our mentor, Churchman, has developed this theory,
but its intellectual roots go back to William James.

James, who is noted for his pioneering book *Psychology*,
and for his development of pragmatism, was also personally affected by archetypical psychology. His memory of the 1906
San Francisco earthquake is a classic example of a normal person's archetypical response to a critical event: "I personified
the earthquake as a permanent individual entity. . . . It came,
moreover, directly to *me*. It stole in behind my neck, and once
inside the room, had me all to itself, and could manifest itself
convincingly. Animus and intent were never more present in
any human action, nor did any human activity ever more defi-
nitely point back to a living agent as its source and origin"
(James, 1911, pp. 209–226).

Among James's outstanding students at Harvard was Ed-
gar A. Singer. Singer became a professor of philosophy at the
University of Pennsylvania, where he further extended the integration of philosophy, psychology, and systems in works such
as *Mind as a Behavior* (1924), *On the Contented Life* (1936),
and *Experience and Reflection* (1959, edited by Churchman
after Singer's death). In these writings, Singer challenges the
simple cause-and-effect model that underlies the mechanistic
worldview. He proposed that the entire universe at one point in
time can serve as the cause of the entire universe at a future
point in time, but that the individual elements are related in a
more complex way. He referred to this relationship as *producer-
product*. A producer is necessary but not sufficient for a product to result. For example, an acorn is one producer of an oak,
but it takes many other producers, such as soil, water, and pro-
tection, for an oak to result. So, too, with the mind, Mitroff
argues. Many stakeholder forces produce personality and behavior.

At Pennsylvania, Singer had a major influence on three of

Mitroff's and my mentors, C. West Churchman, Russell L. Ackoff, and Thomas A. Cowan. In a 1947 book-length manuscript entitled "Psychologistics," Churchman and Ackoff extended Singer's theories, formalized them, and demonstrated how they could be used to control every phase of a well-designed psychological experiment. "Psychologistics" formed a platform on which much of the trio's subsequent work was based. It was a part of Mitroff's experience as well when he studied Singer and Jung with West. Churchman saw in Jung's work a possible explanation of Singer's "heroic mood"—the emotional impetus for breakthroughs in science and technology. Mitroff now has brought these "heroic mood" and teleological concepts together as "stakeholders of the mind."

For me, Mitroff's model is the mind as "drama." Elaborate producer-product chains hover in the background while key characters perform on center stage. It has a certain element of surprise and unpredictability. The result is clearly not mechanical, and yet there is a pattern or plot to it all. The experience is familiar to most of us.

A friend of mine once described her life as a series of "motion pictures." Especially in moments of personal crisis, images of events and people would fly through her head as though they were on film. Occasionally, one of the people would encourage her to do one thing, only to be countermanded by another who said to do something else. Her experience sounds a lot like Mitroff's struggle among stakeholders. My friend spoke of the terror she experienced whenever a "demon" appeared on stage. I think this is an important consideration when one applies Mitroff's approach. When we reach outward and deeply inward for influencing stakeholders, we tend to create anxiety for ourselves. Few terrors are as fearful as those of the unknown, especially the unknown within us. How this affects a person is largely a matter of point of view. Singer evolved his theory as a pathway to personal power, a way to achieve one's potential. Mitroff and I build on this optimism with the concept of stakeholder management (see Mason and Mitroff, 1981).

In this book, Mitroff shows how identifying and forming

productive relationships with one's stakeholders enhances one's personal power. In its essence, this approach is not unlike Paul Tillich's. When faced with anxiety, one must make concrete exactly what the basis of that anxiety is. This converts anxiety into fear, and fear can be met with courage. Tillich called this the "courage to be." It is very much in the spirit of Mitroff's *Stakeholders of the Organizational Mind* as well. Mitroff, following Singer, believes that individuals who understand the forces that affect them can better achieve the potential that lies within them. Mitroff goes further and describes the crucial role archetypes play in the process. In so doing, he creates a potent concept of mind.

Bashō captured the essence of what he saw in haiku. My haiku for this book is

> Mind archetypical
> Timeless characters dancing
> Humanity's tune.

Tucson, Arizona   Richard O. Mason
July 1983

Preface

This book was generated out of at least two intensely conflicting moods. Indeed, the conflict between them mirrors one of the major themes of the book: For all our pretensions to rational self-control, we are the prisoners of our deepest psychic conflicts.

On the one hand, this book was generated out of the excitement, joy, and love of discovering a new way of thinking about inordinately complex human systems and their associated problems. On the other, it was also written out of the most intense mood of dissatisfaction with the current state of managerial and social science. In light of this latter mood, the book represents an unrelenting attack on the superficiality and, at times, nearly total irrelevancy, if not mindlessness, of what passes for research and theory in social and managerial science. It is an intense critique of the artificial, naive, and disastrous separation of the various areas of social science from one another. It argues that we can not achieve a real theoretical understanding of human behavior at any level of society unless we achieve a theory that is informed by what occurs simultaneously at all levels of human behavior.

This book is governed by another fundamental tension, as well. It is written for the reflective practitioner and the reflective theoretician. In particular, it is written for the practitioner and the theoretician of the future, that is, for the manager and the student of tomorrow's organizations. It is hoped that by taking the future into account, this book will be able to serve as an agenda and an outline—not a completed theory—for the development of an entirely new kind of organization theory. It is intended to stimulate thinkers in the social sciences to grapple with issues that for too long have been seriously neglected.

One of the major reasons that much of our current social science is misguided and irrelevant is that it is not concerned with real, complex, messy problems but with small, academic, disciplinary puzzles. Complex, messy problems not only require a very different kind of theorizing but they require a very different kind of tolerance, understanding, and cooperation between both theoreticians and practitioners. Relevant theories cannot be produced by either party acting alone. As John Dewey has emphasized repeatedly, the only distinction worth drawing is not between the practitioner and the theoretician but between good practice and bad practice, good theory and bad theory, reflective theory and practice and unreflective theory and practice.

This book is predicated on a fundamental notion: The problems we face have become so complex that we need, more than ever before, a perspective that allows us to grasp this complexity and to make sense of it. It is also predicated on the notion that those who are charged with managing and studying complex systems can no longer avoid learning a theory of human behavior or, at the very least, being exposed to one, that is adequate to the complexity of the human problems they face constantly. Managers have not balked at learning complex theories of accounting and finance when it has been in their interest. It is now in their direct interest to learn theories of human behavior that can help them deal with the enormously complex human dilemmas with which they are continually beset. If only in part, such theories must be based on psychoanalytic ideas. However fragmented, incomplete, and contradictory they may be, the diverse theories of psychoanalysis developed by such pioneering giants as Freud and Jung represent the most serious and best attempts to date to deal with the enormous complexities and subtleties of human behavior. To be of interest and relevance to the practitioner, student, and teacher of management, however, the insights and theories of Freud and Jung must be translated into the theory and practice of management and their potential usefulness in this area must be demonstrated. This is one of my primary aims in this book.

Acknowledgments

No book is ever the product of a single mind; this point is generally true, but it is especially applicable to a book on the nature of the mind. The minds that have shaped and influenced mine are too numerous to name. In line with one of the principal theses of this book, I could never be consciously aware of them all. However, several of my colleagues offered extensive comments on an early draft of this book. I wish to acknowledge how much I appreciate their help, even though I was not always wise enough to follow their advice: Per-Olof Berg, Raul Carvajal, Daryl Chubin, Jody Fry, Craig Lundberg, Joanne Martin, Gareth Morgan, Kurt Motamedi, Mark Pastin, Peter Reason, Seymour Sarason, William Torbert, and Gordon Walter. In particular, I wish to acknowledge the tremendous influence of my closest personal friends and colleagues: Vincent P. Barabba, Warren Bennis, William Dunn, Ralph Kilmann, and Richard Mason. Richard Mason's Foreword is an indication of how long and far we have traveled together. Thanks, Richard.

Above all, I am deeply indebted to my teachers, C. West Churchman, Thomas A. Cowan, and Russell L. Ackoff. They have provided me with a lifetime of inspiration. They are responsible for the method in my madness and for a lot of the madness as well.

Finally, there are two of the most colorful and interesting characters I have ever met, my wife, Donna, and my daughter, Dana. I love them for that and much, much more.

Los Angeles, California   Ian I. Mitroff
July 1983

Contents

The Author

Ian I. Mitroff is Harold Quinton Distinguished Professor of Business Policy in the Graduate School of Business at the University of Southern California. He received the B.S. degree in engineering physics (1961), the M.S. degree in structural engineering (1963), and the Ph.D. degree in engineering psychology (1967), with a strong minor in the philosophy of social science, all from the University of California at Berkeley.

He is a member of the American Association for the Advancement of Science, the American Psychological Association, the American Sociological Association, the Institute of Management Science, the Philosophy of Science Association, and the American Academy of Management.

He has published over one hundred articles and books in professional journals and popular magazines. Above all, he is interested in the relationship of theory to managerial practice and practice to theory. He is especially concerned with the development of theories of social science that are of direct interest and relevance to practitioners. He no longer believes that the gap between theory and practice is relevant to the kind of world in which we live.

Stakeholders
of the
Organizational Mind

*Toward a New View
of Organizational
Policy Making*

CHAPTER ONE

Introduction:
The Stakeholder Concept

This book attempts to bridge and to heal one of the most fundamental divisions in the social sciences: the strict separation between where the *inside* of the autonomous individual supposedly leaves off and where the *outside* of the collective or society supposedly begins. Above all, it is particularly concerned with providing a perspective that as much as possible attempts to heal the severe fragmentation and dissociation to which the spirit of Western man has been subjected.

To accomplish this necessitates that we explore the thoughts of some of the most insightful social scientists that Western culture has produced. As incredible as it is, for the most part the writings of these powerful thinkers have been virtually ignored in the thinking of current theorists of institutions, organizations, and policy making. *Ignored* may not be the appropriate word in this context. A better phrase might be "not even recognized in the first place." For all practical purposes these writings are virtually nonexistent from the standpoint of those fields of knowledge concerned with institutions, organizations, and policy making. Some of the most profound theorists of the human psyche and of human behavior have not been given the consideration due them by those fields of human be-

1

havior that could, paradoxically enough, benefit most from their considerable insights.

The particular theorists to whom this book is especially indebted are Bruno Bettelheim, Norman O. Brown, Joseph Campbell, Sigmund Freud, James Hillman, Julian Jaynes, Carl Gustav Jung, Herbert Marcuse, Erich Neumann, Marie-Louise von Franz, and Ken Wilber. While the collective works of all of these preeminent thinkers touch on nearly every one of the various social sciences, they all share a major interest. They are interested in the development, extension, reinterpretation, and application of psychoanalytic ideas in one form or another to the problem of the individual self in society.

Freud and Jung of course need no introduction. They are two of the founding giants of psychoanalysis. Bruno Bettelheim is a distinguished professor emeritus of education, psychology, and psychiatry at the University of Chicago. He is widely known for his many writings but perhaps especially those examining fairy tales from a psychoanalytic viewpoint. Norman O. Brown is a professor of classics at the University of California at Santa Cruz. His book *Life Against Death* (1959) achieved widespread fame. It was hailed as an important critical examination of psychoanalytic thought from the vantage point of an extremely broad view of Western culture. Joseph Campbell, a world-renowned student of mythology, has taught for many years at Sarah Lawrence College. He is hailed for his many writings which have made the reading and interpretation of myths accessible to both the academic specialist and the public at large. James Hillman is a Jungian analyst who now teaches at the University of Dallas. For years he was head of research at the Jungian Institute in Zurich, Switzerland. Along with his former colleague Marie-Louise von Franz (who still resides in Switzerland), he has pushed the theory and interpretation of archetypes deeper and further. Julian Jaynes is a professor of psychology at Princeton University. Trained as a behaviorist, he has moved far beyond the confines of traditional academic psychology to speculate on the origin of consciousness of early man. Herbert Marcuse was a social philosopher of immense influence. As one of the members of the Frankfurt school of social theory, he combined philosophy and social theory to show how each not only depended on but also enriched the other. He was especially concerned with the philosophical and theoretical foundations of psychoanalysis. Erich Neumann was a Jungian analyst of immense influence. He produced some of the most powerful in-depth theoretical analyses of the function of archetypes in the human psyche. Marie-Louise von Franz is a Jungian analyst and scholar. She is widely known for her brilliant analyses of archetypes in fairy tales. Finally, Ken Wilber is a young scholar of immense potential. He has already produced a highly significant set of books that explore the notion of mind across both Western and Eastern viewpoints.

The work of every one of these individuals exemplifies a standard to which this book aspires: the construction of a multifaceted, richly variegated theory of human behavior. Their work achieves this because they dared to cross over and to break free of tight sacrosanct disciplinary boundaries. As a whole their work touches on such fields as anthropology, neurology, psychology, economics, history, mythology, philosophy, comparative and world religions, and theology.

The work of these leading pioneers constantly illuminates the proposition that the mind of the individual and the culture of the surrounding social environment are so constantly intertwined, so intimately bound up with one another, that it is virtually impossible to say with any great precision where the one begins and the other leaves off. In fact, precision is often dangerous in that it adds to the confusion that the distinction is real. The distinctions between the individual, the group, and society are conceptual at best, not actual.

It needs to be especially stressed that although the initial point of departure, that is, the origin, of many of the ideas in this book is psychoanalytic, it is not necessarily their point of destination. While many of the ideas that are used derive historically from psychoanalysis, psychoanalytic theory per se is not my primary concern. In this sense, this book is neither basically Freudian nor Jungian although I draw heavily upon the work of both men. My primary concern is with the creation of a new way of studying and understanding the deeper features of human systems, that is, the motives for human behavior that lie deeper than those the current main body of organization theory treats or is able to account for. Psychoanalytic theory is at the very least highly relevant to this aim, for psychoanalysis is one of the very few human sciences that deliberately seeks out the deeper underlying aspects of human behavior and aspires to construct a satisfying explanation of it.

To be of relevance, however, to such concerns as modern organization theory and institutional and policy analysis, psychoanalytic ideas need to be recast so that their contribution is more directly apparent to theorists and practitioners alike. This recasting is one of the major aims of this book.

My colleagues and I (see Mason and Mitroff, 1981) believe that we have discovered a simple yet effective way of communicating the insights and theories of Freud, Jung, and others on our list, and of integrating them into a comprehensive framework for analyzing and managing complex human systems. This framework or perspective is the subject of this book.

Why should students of organizations and those whom I call *reflective managers* be interested in such an approach and what does it promise to do for them? There are a number of responses to this question. The first is that whether or not it is liked, the modern large-scale corporation is buffeted by a growing disparate array of forces, many of which seem increasingly beyond its control. Along with many others, I call these forces *stakeholders* in contrast to the more limited term *stockholder*. Stakeholders are all those interest groups, parties, actors, claimants, and institutions—both internal and external to the corporation—that exert a hold on it. That is, stakeholders are all those parties who either affect or who are affected by a corporation's actions, behavior, and policies. Stakeholders typically comprise a much larger group than does the more limited class of claimants known as stockholders. The stockholders are only one of many competing and diverse groups that impact on the modern corporation, organization, or institution and must increasingly be considered by it if it is to survive, that is, if it is to assume control of its destiny.

In the book *Challenging Strategic Planning Assumptions*

(1981), Richard O. Mason and I show how to identify major social system stakeholders and how to assess their impact on public as well as private organizations. The result is a method that is both practical and theoretical for dealing with complex, messy, real-world problems, that is, problems for which there are often many equally promising solutions and not just one "best" solution that is accepted as such by all stakeholders. The point is that different stakeholders do not generally share the same definition of an organization's "problems," and hence, they do not in general share the same "solutions." As a result, the typical approaches to organizational problem solving, which generally presuppose prior consensus or agreement among parties, cannot be used; they break down. Instead, a method is needed that builds off a starting point of disagreement—indeed, regards such initial disagreement as a strength since it informs us of different options—and works toward a final point of shared commitment to a set of possible solution alternatives. This, in brief, was the message of our earlier book on challenging assumptions.

This volume carries this effort much further into the social sciences as a whole. It shows that there are broader and deeper classes of stakeholders that influence the behavior of managers in organizations and the behavior of organizations themselves. In a word, the individual human psyche or personality may itself be construed as a miniature social system, as a "plurality of selves." While Freud, Jung, and the other thinkers to whom I am indebted may differ as to the nature of these selves, all would probably agree that these selves exert a considerable influence on how individuals act in groups and in organizations.

Where organizational sociology in particular and political science and sociology in general treat stakeholders that are *external* to the skin of a given individual in society, psychoanalysis and depth psychology treat *internal* stakeholders—those that constitute the innermost core of the individual's psyche. The major thesis of this book is that there is a constant interaction, overlap, and interplay between these two broad classes of stakeholders, internal and external to the individual, the organization, the institution, and the state. The concept of stakeholders, suitably framed, provides a way of seeing the various social sciences in tandem, not in opposition to one another. Which science has the sole right to treat which kind of stakeholder is less relevant under the framework of social analysis developed in this book. To repeat, my concern is not with traditional psychoanalysis, psychology, sociology, and so forth, per se, but with using these disciplines as a jumping off point for formulating a nontraditional method of psychosocial system analysis.

To give an example of what I am after, consider the fact that every organization has some form of competition. Further, it is not clear that an organization would be better off without any form of competition. To remove competition would be to rob an organization of a significant part of its motivation to change, improve, and so on. Thus, the general term *competitor* describes one of the most important stakeholders that every organization has and must consider in both its current and future plans and policies. One must always ask: "What is my current competition like? If I do such and such, what will they do, and vice versa? Further, what might my future competition be like?" Not to ask, not to even consider, these and other kinds of questions is to commit organizational suicide.

Between the first and final drafts of this book, an incident occurred that shows only too well the vital importance of considering stakeholders. The incident is actually a series of events: the poisoning of the products of several drug companies. These incidents reveal that every organization is now extremely vulnerable to any one of a host of evil stakeholders. It also shows that every organization has a "shadow side" that is extremely difficult, if not almost impossible, to deal with. The shadow side is revealed in the fact that products originally designed to do good, that is, to cure, can be utilized by evil parties to do just the opposite. As recent events show, organizations are not equipped to deal with such forces. As Chapter Two shows, one can deal with such forces if one has a revamped image of what "dealing with" means and an appropriate method for assisting in this venture.

Here is where a psychoanalytically based theory of management comes in and makes a fundamental contribution to our practice and understanding of management. An organization's concept of its competition can never be based purely on facts alone. Further, it can never be the same for all parties (stakeholders) internal to the organization. The reason is that people differ in their emotional makeup and psychological structure. They perceive the same "facts" differently, if not seeing entirely different facts to begin with. As a result, one *projects* an aspect of one's internal psyche onto one's external competition. The competition is colored, tainted, so to speak, by that projection. Unless one has some minimal awareness of how such psychological projections occur and why, one is in danger of perceiving one's competitors to be more evil than they are or of perceiving them to be more benign than they are. One's concept of one's competitors will be psychologically infected or contaminated.

What is true of the single stakeholder "competitor" is true of all the stakeholders that constitute the complex social system in which the modern corporation is embedded. An important purpose of the present book is thus: (1) to give managers and theoreticians a broader understanding of the psychosocial system that surrounds them and of which they are a part and (2) to provide both with a framework that helps them to manage, to understand, and to cope with the complexity of this psychosocial system—if only a little bit better.

This is not a book of ordinary social science. Its story of human understanding does not include the point of view of the passionless, disinterested observer of human affairs (Mitroff, 1974; Mitroff and Kilmann, 1978). The author is not a neutral, dispassionate observer of the social world. Neither does he believe that others are. The book is intended to show how one can confront the stories we invent to cope with the multitude of social worlds that touch all of us the oftener and the more steadily we reflect on them.

Outline of the Book

Because the theory we are about to explore is involved, it is helpful to present an overview of the entire book. Chapter Two presents the synopsis of an actual case in corporate policy making on which my colleagues and I have worked. The basic point of the case is not the treatment and resolution of the particular substantive issues at hand but rather how the case was approached. The case illustrates how we discovered and evolved a very special methodology for treating highly ill-structured, complex, messy, real-world problems. The case and the methodology show how the notion of stakeholders naturally arises in the course of considering important real-world problems. The case also reveals the existence of the basic entities—stakeholders and their associated properties—that are at the core of a methodology for treating ill-structured problems.

While originally developed and formulated for treating problems at the institutional, sociological, or policy level, the chapter provides the basis for a methodology for treating ill-structured problems at whatever level of human system analysis from which they arise. In Chapter Nine, I discuss how the methodology applies to the treatment of ill-structured problems at the intrapsychic level as well as the extrapsychic levels. The methodology is perfectly general once it is realized that we are simultaneously treating stakeholders and their associated properties at varying levels of social reality.

Where Chapter Two introduces the concept of stakeholders via a concrete but particular case, Chapter Three shows that there are a number of definite methods for systematically identifying stakeholders and their attendant properties. It is not enough, in other words, to contend that every social system, at any level, can be viewed as composed of stakeholders. One must show how the notion of stakeholders is grounded in some basic concepts (theories) with regard to the fundamental structure of social systems. This is the purpose of Chapter Three.

Chapter Three does not show how to identify stakeholders at every level at which human systems operate. It shows only how to identify those stakeholders at the institutional, sociological, or policy level of analysis. Chapter Three thus treats what conventional or contemporary sociology has to offer regarding the identification of stakeholders at the kinds and levels of social system analysis with which it deals. In a word, the chapter shows how to identify those stakeholders *external* to the skin of the autonomous individual personality.

Chapter Three reveals a defect of our entire mode of analysis. The methods for identifying stakeholders and the kinds of properties that can be associated with them read after awhile like laundry lists. One asks: "What is the connection between the items? How do they hang together? What is the underlying theory that ties them together?" The chapter shows that at the present we lack such a theory. This is precisely what makes the analysis and treatment of social systems indeterminate or in the language of this book, "messy." One of the basic points of the chapter is that unless we are willing to make some very strong assumptions whose plausibility is in principle just as open to question and to challenge as those assumptions we are using the theory to uncover, we can not proceed further. To proceed further we would need a theory that makes recourse to deeper assumptions regarding human behavior than current sociological theory supplies. We can not treat the so-called various levels of human behavior as rigidly distinct or neatly separable from one another. Each mode of social analysis presupposes, and more often than not without its either knowing or acknowledging it, fundamental knowledge from all the other levels of social analysis it so easily dismisses. The best we can do is to use these other levels to illuminate the catalogue of assumptions that enter into the construction of social theories and the management of social systems.

Chapters Four and Five begin our first treatment of "stakeholders within the skin," or in the psyche, of the individual. Personality types delineated by Carl Jung and Eric Berne are used as starting points for a treatment of those stakeholders that constitute the most easily visible, surface or egoic, aspects of the mind. Chapter Five in particular also shows how the personality typologies developed by Jung and Berne can be overlaid to give a richer understanding of ego-state psychology.

Chapters Four and Five also show how the ideas of Jung and Berne are of direct concern and interest to the fields of management and organizational behavior. As different types of individuals have different kinds of personalities, different types of organizations have different personalities or styles as well. The personalities of individuals affect the design and structure of organizations including what they recognize as valid information on which to base their decisions.

Society and the minds of the individuals in it can be thought of as a giant sphere. The extreme outermost layers of the sphere are composed of those stakeholders that constitute society, that is, banks or financial institutions, universities, transportation companies, in short all the institutions that in general make up a complex modern society. Chapters Two and Three treat stakeholders at this level. At the next layer down inside the sphere are to be found the psyches of concrete individuals. Chapters Four through Six treat stakeholders at this level. The difference between these chapters is that where Chapters Four and Five treat those aspects of the individual psyche that are closest to the stakeholders as discussed in Chapters Two and Three (that is, institutional and sociological stakeholders), Chapter Six treats those stakeholders that constitute the deepest layers of the mind and hence the very innermost core of the sphere, to pursue this metaphor to its extreme.

Chapter Six treats the strangest of all the stakeholders of the mind—archetypes. Archetypes are the most extreme, purest symbols that the mind is capable of producing and of experiencing of itself and everything else that constitutes the world. Some typical examples of archetypes are Christ, perfection or completeness often symbolized by a circle or a mandala, fire, water, and so forth. Archetypes seem truly universal in that they are revealed in all the Great Dreams (that is, religions, mythologies, and writings) of all cultures.

Chapter Six shows that the properties that archetypes obey are drastically different from the properties of the other kinds of stakeholders which have been encountered in previous chapters. Chapter Six also attempts to show how archetypes can infuse and infect stakeholders at any and all levels simultaneously. In this sense, if the sphere model or metaphor for the mind is an apt one, then it is a very strange kind of sphere indeed. *It is a sphere wherein every point is inherently on the inside and outside all at once.* It is more akin to a holographic sphere than a sphere of ordinary everyday life.

Chapter Seven presents several contemporary examples of

real-life archetypes in action. Because of the somewhat difficult but necessary theoretical nature of Chapter Six, it is necessary to give some concrete examples of archetypes and to show how they are capable of influencing everyday life. Archetypes are not solely or necessarily confined to the pursuits of esoteric scholars. In more ways than one, it is a shame that those who have spent their lives studying archetypes have not felt it necessary to relate the fruits of their labors to the affairs of everyday people. Chapter Seven attempts to do this by showing that the influence of archetypes can be found everywhere. This chapter is thus an attempt to make the concept more accessible to a nonspecialized audience and to show its relevance for social analysis.

Stakeholders do not exist by themselves or in isolation from one another. Furthermore, the properties of stakeholders, particularly archetypes, do not transpire in dry, abstract lists. They are part of the working, living culture of civilizations, institutions, and the psyches of individuals. More often than not, the properties are revealed in terms of stories. Chapter Eight analyzes the differences in kind between the stories that (1) science (as a representative of impersonal institutional analysis), (2) ego-state psychology, and (3) archetypal psychology (as a representative of highly personalized, individuated analysis) tell about the world. The differences and the similarities among these three different ways to tell the story of nature and humanity's place in it are compared and contrasted. The comparison sheds additional light on the nature of stakeholders at different levels of existence and of social analysis.

By the kind of fundamental investigation it is, any in-depth analysis of the nature of social reality must obviously deal explicitly with philosophical concerns at some point or another. Chapter Nine raises a number of fundamental questions: "What is a proper method for studying archetypes in social life? Is there some hierarchy or evolution of archetypes? What is the relationship between archetypes and the psychosocial evolution of man? What entirely new kinds of organization theory and radically new kinds of organizations does the study of archetypes open up?" Finally, the last chapter briefly summarizes and recapitulates some of our main findings and conclusions.

As stated previously, this is not a book of ordinary social science. It does not believe that the social sciences fundamentally are either like the physical sciences or that the attempt should be made to make them appear so. To attempt to do so fundamentally distorts the essential nature of our subject matter— the psychosocial nature of human institutions and of the human psyche.

This book also differs in that it believes that the social sciences have already produced their Newtons and their Einsteins. Only they are not Newtons and Einsteins in the conventional senses of those terms. They are not mechanicians of society. Their aim is not to give impersonal, disinterested mathematical descriptions of human behavior but rather to give a glimpse into the deepest recesses of the soul. As such, none of them is afraid to use the term *soul*. The Newtons and the Einsteins of social science to whom I am referring are among the eleven guides listed earlier. However, since Newton and Einstein have by now become archetypes of superior attainment in *physical* science, we will have to find other archetypal figures uniquely suited to symbolize social science as I conceive of it. This is the journey on which we are about to embark.

CHAPTER TWO

Analyzing Corporate Policy Making

Assumptions are the building blocks of a person's makeup and therefore of behavior. . . . Assumptions guide the individual, determine what he or she will and will not do. They determine what the person expects or anticipates from self and others in any situation [Anderson, 1981, p. 779].

The better one understands one's assumptions, the better able one can be to change behavior and thus avoid trouble [Anderson, 1981, p. 781].

The Case of the Drug Company

Imagine that you are the chief executive of a large organization and that you are faced with a problem that threatens to wipe out your entire business. This is a problem that would certainly command your attention! The problem is this (actually, as we shall see, there are several levels to the problem): You produce a product, a painkiller, which because it has a narcotic base can be obtained only by prescription through a physician. Upon obtaining the prescription for your drug, a well-known brand-name product, the patient takes it to his or her favorite pharmacist. The pharmacist, in turn, either fills it without com-

13

ment as instructed by the physician or says something to the patient like, "Did you know that there is a generic-brand substitute available for the drug your physician has prescribed at a much lower cost than the brand-name? If you like, I can substitute the cheaper generic brand for the more expensive brand label. Which do you prefer I do?" And indeed, in some states the pharmacist is required by law to inform the patient.

This action while potentially beneficial to the patient, *assuming* that the generic-brand drug is of equal quality to the name-brand drug, is a potential financial disaster for the drug company. It threatens to wipe out one of the mainstay products of the company. Since the drug annually generates millions of dollars for the company, the company's whole financial structure is threatened as a result. What do you as the chief executive officer do?

You can do a number of things. You can attempt to think the problem through yourself, taking the whole thing upon yourself, either not delegating it to anyone else or not trusting it to them. You can then attempt to choose on your own the best option open to you to combat the threat. Or there is something else you can do which depending how it is done can either replace or supplement the first alternative of going it alone. This is to involve others in the analysis of the problem. Since the problem threatens financial disaster for the whole organization, it might be desirable to involve others in a consideration of their own fate for the good of the whole. Also, it just might be that more heads are better than one in coming up with needed and creative alternatives, especially in a crisis situation when critical faculties are likely to be blunted. No one mind can ever know all there is to know about any complex organization. It is the height of folly and delusion to fool oneself into thinking that one can. The final decision will still be yours, but if you have the right style of management (really, personality), this need not preclude participation by others in the analysis of the problem and perhaps even in the final decision. Certainly you would like others to go along with whatever you decide and not to sabotage it.

In this real-world case the chief executive decided to involve some of his senior executives in the analysis of the problem. Because of the critical nature of the problem, it impacted on every aspect of the business. As a result, the chief executive officer (CEO) felt that he not only had no choice but to solicit the most widespread expert advice from as many different aspects of the organization as possible but that he should actually welcome such diversity. The problem was too critical not to consult with others. As a consequence, twelve or so executives representing all of the diverse aspects of the business were assembled and asked to advise the CEO. Here is precisely where the deeper aspects of the problem began to emerge.

A strange thing began to happen. The twelve executives split into three subfactions. This was not done out of any animosity among them, but because complex problems naturally suggest more than one best alternative. The groups began to coalesce around particular alternatives. Each group then proceeded to make the best, that is, strongest, case for its alternative to the exclusion of the other two.

The three alternatives were as follows: The first group wanted to lower the price of the drug; the second wanted to raise the price; and the third wanted to keep it the same. The first group in effect wanted to "out-generic" the generic drug by making the company's drug into a generic, at least in terms of price. This alternative or policy is the one that most easily occurs to anyone. It is in many ways a defensive policy. This does not necessarily make it wrong, for as we shall see, in complex real-world problems the right or wrong answers are not always clear. Some responses may be stronger than others along some grounds, but very rarely is one alternative strongest or best on all dimensions.

In the realm of complex problems not only is there usually more than one serious alternative but, further still, there is generally at least one pair of alternatives such that each part of the pair is the complete opposite of the other. Thus, in the case at hand, the second alternative is the diametrical opposite of the first.

The reasoning behind alternative two is even more fascinating and important for our purposes. The group of executives that supported this alternative argued that faced with the threat of generic drugs they had to do something that would communicate to the marketplace the difference between their drug and the others. In short they had to differentiate themselves from the mass. This group felt that by raising the price of the drug they would be communicating increased confidence in the *quality* of their product to the marketplace.

The last group argued something entirely different. While the first two groups were oriented toward the external marketplace and the price consumers would be willing to pay or to bear, the last group was oriented toward cutting internal costs of production. They argued that if the price of the drug were maintained at current levels or, at the very least, set midway between the proposals of the first two groups, then they could raise profits by cutting internal costs. They proposed to do this by eliminating the research and development (R and D) arm of the company, the largest source of internal costs to the company and perhaps to drug companies in general. Their argument was that if the current price of the drug was sufficient to generate necessary revenue for the company, that is if the demand for the drug remained stable, then the company would not need to develop new products. To say the least, the R and D department would not be overjoyed with this, but then business was business, at least as this group saw it.

Since each group was of roughly equal power in the organization, no group could force through its pet alternative over the objections of the other. Each group had to convince all the groups if the company was to embark on a unified course of action that everyone could embrace with confidence.

How then did the groups try to persuade one another of the correctness of the policy each one espoused? They did what most managers have been trained to do. They analyzed past data, for example, the past sales volume (amount sold) for various selling prices of the drug, and where they could, they collected new data from, for example, trade magazines and reports from salespeople in the field. The trouble was, in this case at least, that the data did not settle anything. It actually made things worse by intensifying the proponents' commitments to their separate policies. The reason for this may be the most illuminating and instructive aspect of the entire case.

One of the valuable things we learn in school is to test our ideas against the criticisms of others and, wherever possible, challenge data from the outside world. In school this tactic generally succeeds because the problems that are presented to the student are so greatly simplified. Indeed, some would say that what are presented under the guise of problems are really exercises and not problems at all (Ackoff, 1974). An exercise is something that typically has a single correct solution and, furthermore, when it is arrived at it is recognized as such by all parties. There is usually very little uncertainty as to whether or not one has reached the right solution. Problems, in contrast, may have many different solutions because they may be looked at from different, equally valid, angles. Deeper still, unlike exercises, problems do not have the same meaning for different parties. That is, in an exercise, we can be relatively confident that each party starts from the same set of givens, that is, the same definition of the exercise to be solved. In a problem by contrast we can not share this basic confidence. Witness the problem we have been discussing. The problem is not the same for all parties because each interprets it from very different grounds, defining the basic problem somewhat differently.

More data merely confounded the mess with which management was faced. And *mess* is indeed a more appropriate word to use in describing this case than the more benign word *problem*. Ackoff (1974) defines a mess as a system of problems none of which can easily be separated from one another. The case was not an example of a nice, neat, clean exercise that is found at the end of most textbooks, wherein the student is typically given everything one needs to find the single right answer. Instead, each group was assuming different things about the nature of the problem. Each group was taking certain things for granted, to be true, without conscious or explicit knowledge.

As a result, each group was selectively reinterpreting the data they all shared in common, unconsciously of course, to suit, if not prove, its case. Further, if past common data were lacking and hence new data had to be collected, each group was collecting different data from different sources. Each source was designed, again unconsciously, to prove each group's case. Hence, *instead of data being used to test each alternative, believers in each alternative were procuring data that would confirm its validity.* A very circular process indeed and one from which management had tried repeatedly—without success—to extricate itself. But since everything depended upon which assumptions were made, as in fact every case does, the case could not be analyzed without making some very important critical assumptions. But since very few, if any, of the assumptions were ever brought to the surface for conscious inspection and challenge, each group cycled around its own vicious circle.

Not that management did not try to break out of this circle. They used every financial model and approach of which they were aware in an attempt to get some neutral piece of data or critical finding that would once and for all clearly differentiate among the alternatives. However much they tried, time and again their efforts failed.

It was at this point that James Emshoff and I were called upon to consult. For years, Emshoff and I had worked on problems of this kind independent of one another. I spent a year in a visiting appointment at the Wharton School of Finance, University of Pennsylvania, which gave us the opportunity to combine our insights. As a result of this collaboration, we achieved what for us was a real breakthrough (a much overused word) in formulating a method for handling problems of the kind we have been describing. We were able to formulate in practical and operational terms a viable method for handling complex, messy problems.

Since the method has been described extensively elsewhere, I shall merely review it here (see Mason and Mitroff, 1981). The nature of the review is designed to show how a new concept of managing complex systems that is based on psychoanalytic ideas naturally grows out of our initial method.

Assumption Analysis

It soon became clear to Emshoff and me that differences in basic assumptions were at the heart of the disagreement between the groups of executives in the drug company. Each group was making fundamentally different assumptions about the real nature of the problem. No wonder more data did not settle anything between them. More data only served to activate underlying differences. It did not test or resolve them, it only made things worse. We have a perfect example of where more can lead to less. Since for the most part the assumptions remained buried and implicit, the groups themselves were largely unaware of what was happening. All they knew was that time and again they disagreed and were immensely frustrated.

How then could we get the participants to reveal to us and to themselves in a nonthreatening way the underlying assumptions that were driving their policies? Assumptions are like the weather. Everyone talks about them, their influence, their crucial importance but, after that, no one offers a way of getting to them and dealing with them. This is what we were after. Having said this, I am not sure that we ourselves were fully aware of what we were fashioning in the initial meetings with the drug company executives, but it soon began to dawn on us.

It turned out that both Emshoff and I had for some time been working with the concept of *stakeholders*, which was very close to the idea of assumptions. The stakeholder concept emanates out of our concept and that of others regarding the fundamental constitution and operation of complex social systems. Figures 1 and 2 show these relationships.

Figure 1 shows what we refer to as the "Milton Friedman view of the world." It says essentially that there are only three major players in the game of business: stockholders, customers, and the company itself. According to Friedman, the major, if not sole, responsibility of the company is to the stockholders, who provide the initial working capital to start the business and to keep it going. In turn, the stockholders expect to get back profits in the form of dividends. The customers are at the opposite end of this relationship. They receive goods, services, or products from the company. In turn, they provide income to the company in the form of sales. According to this story, in many ways the company functions as a middleman.

This interaction, whether according to Friedman or oth-

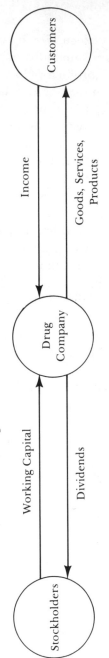

Figure 1. A Traditional Stakeholder Map.

Figure 2. An Expanded Stakeholder Map.

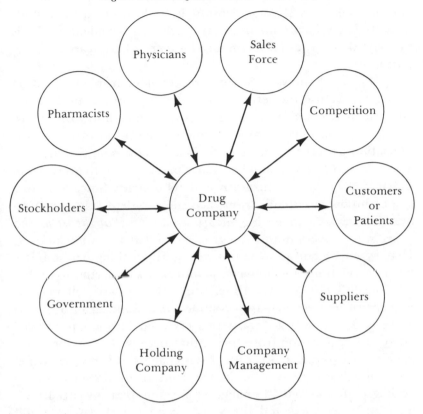

ers, is vastly more complicated than the diagram implies. But in its bare essentials, this is the traditional image of the corporation: It either is or should be beholden largely to the stockholders, and the firm's sole responsibility is to make a profit, not to engage in social actions or reform. The stakeholder theory of the firm challenges all of this.

According to the stakeholder concept, the modern organization—whether public or private—is beholden to, at the very least is affected by, a larger set of forces than the three parties, stockholders, customers, and the organization itself. While none of them is formally a part of the organization, these other forces or parties affect its internal policies and external behavior nonetheless. Even more important, not to *systematically* take into account how an organization is both affected by and affects its larger environment, particularly in a turbulent world, is to court disaster, as all too many industries have learned in recent years.

Figure 2 shows a broader stakeholder map of the drug company. We use the term *stakeholder* to connote all those individual actors and parties, organized groups and professions, and institutions that have a bearing on the behavior of the organization as revealed in its policies and actions on the environment. In short, a stakeholder is any party that both affects and is affected by an organization and its policies. Since a double line of influence extends from each stakeholder to the organization and back again, *an organization may be thought of as the entire set of relationships it has with itself and its stakeholders.* That is, an organization is not necessarily a thing per se but a series of relationships between a wide series of parties. As these relationships change over time, the organization itself may be thought of as changing, as becoming a different organization, as it were. The failure to grasp this essential fact has prevented many an organization from seeing that because its environment, that is, its external stakeholders, has changed it is not the same, even though internally it looks the same to itself. Since we are dealing with a system, a change in any one part potentially affects all other parts and the whole system itself (Ackoff and Emery, 1974).

Let us examine Figure 2 a bit further to see its implications. Every organization has some form of external competition. While not formally a part of the organization, it affects the organization and its policies nonetheless. Every organization must ask itself such questions as: "If we do such and such, what will our competition do? If we enter this market, will our competition grow, leave, retaliate? Who is our current competition? How determined, how strong are they? What might our future competition be? Can we prevent our competition from entering our market in the first place? Can we raise the entry costs (for example, capital accumulation) high enough to keep them out or at least block their easy entry? If we decide, for whatever reasons, to get out of a particular market, can we do it in such a way as to make it more difficult for our competition to get out of a worsening situation? That is, if we get out first, will it be more difficult for others to get out later?" These questions are so important that an exciting major school of business policy and planning has arisen recently to consider them explicitly (Porter, 1980).

Competition is certainly an important factor in the present case since it was the explicit threat from lower-price generic drugs that started the whole crisis in the first place. But so are all the other stakeholder parties. The company's sales force is an important stakeholder since whatever policy the company enacts potentially affects its commissions and hence its motivation to sell the drug. Physicians and pharmacists are also obviously important since it is they and not the drug company who have direct contact with the customers—the patient, in this case. Their behavior, that is, their attitude toward the company and its products, is obviously an important factor in the patient's behavior.

Let us consider just a few more stakeholders. Government is a stakeholder in this case in at least two important roles. First, through the Federal Drug Administration, it regulates the sale, release, testing, use, and distribution of drugs. This is especially the case where narcotics are involved. Second, since the drug has an important narcotic base, the government comes into the picture through the procurement and regulation of opiates from foreign countries. Things that happen in poppy fields a long way from home affect a drug company here in the United States.

Finally, consider the stakeholder holding company. The drug company in this case was owned by another larger pharmaceutical company fifty miles up the road, so to speak. They certainly had a stake in whatever the subsidiary decided to do for it would certainly affect the profits of the larger parent company.

What has all this got to do with assumptions? Simply put, *assumptions are the properties of stakeholders.* The proponents of the different policies in the drug company were disagreeing—

often violently—because they were positing very different properties about the behavior of the stakeholders. But why assumptions? Because no one had the definitive data, information, or
arguments to know beyond all doubt what all the stakeholders
were like or how they were likely to behave in all situations.
The bigger, more complex the problem, the more it is likely to
involve a wider array of stakeholder forces. As a result, the
more the assumptions that will have to be made. It is a characteristic, fundamental feature of real-world, as opposed to textbook, problems that not everything of basic importance can be
known prior to working on the problem. In the real world we
do not start with a clear statement of the problem before we
commence working on it. Rather, a statement of the problem
often emerges only with difficulty over time and only as a direct result of our working on the problem. Very few problems
come directly to us preformulated from the gods. Rather, they
are intensely human creations born out of the process of what it
means to be human, that is, human interaction.

At last we come to the crux of the problem. Let us take
the single stakeholder, the physician, and illustrate what was
driving the groups apart. And indeed, it turns out that the assumptions that were made about the physician were the most
critical. For ease of presentation, we shall consider only two
groups, the one that wanted to raise the price of the drug and
the one that wanted to lower it. The group that wanted to raise
the price was assuming implicitly that physicians were moti-
vated primarily by the traditional medical model, that is, that
physicians were primarily concerned with the health and well-
being of the patient relatively irrespective of cost. That is, this
group was assuming that physicians were relatively price-insensitive. Physicians would prescribe the drug if they thought it
would do the job, that is, they were convinced of its quality
and, if they did, their recommendation would be critical in
overcoming the counter-suggestion of the pharmacist. As one
can see, there are actually a whole bundle of assumptions tied
up with the physician and his or her effect on other stakeholders, such as the patient and the pharmacist.

The group that wanted to lower the price of the drug was

assuming implicitly that because of the skyrocketing cost of medical care, physicians were becoming more cost conscious than ever before. In other words, they assumed that physicians were becoming increasingly price-sensitive and would no longer prescribe a drug merely on the basis of quality and irrespective of cost. At some point, quality, especially claimed superior quality, would have to give way to cost.

There was a special wrinkle that Emshoff and I introduced that made it possible for the different groups to be able to see not only their assumptions but also the effects of their assumptions. This was the introduction of a simple yet effective way of mapping or plotting assumptions. (See Figure 3.)

Figure 3. A Grid for Charting Stakeholder Assumptions.

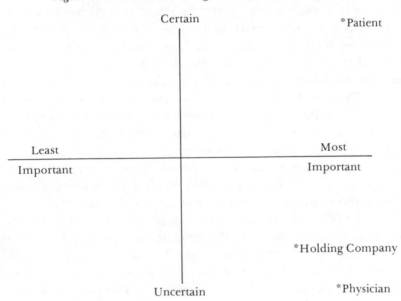

Once the pertinent stakeholders have been identified and the assumptions associated with them have been surfaced, typically some assumptions are more critical or important to the success or viability of a policy than others. Likewise, one feels more confident about the truth or certainty of some assumptions than others. Thus, Figure 3 shows that all of the groups, but for very different reasons, regarded the physician as the most important but most uncertain stakeholder. Consider again the high-price group and understand that *it is the assumption with regard to the stakeholder, not the stakeholder itself, that is being plotted in Figure 3.* Thus, while the assumption that physicians are price-insensitive is the most critical (important) assumption to the success of the high-price group's policy, when revealed, it is also the one that is the most uncertain. Without the assumption of price-insensitivity this group's policy can not be successful but at the same time it is the most open to doubt. Are all physicians price-insensitive? Or merely some? If so, what are the "some" who are price-insensitive like? What are their personal and demographic characteristics? No wonder more data did not settle anything; the data that were relevant to these questions were either unavailable—they had never been collected before—or they were ambiguous. One could infer whatever one wanted from the data because the data that were available were all mixed up; they contained data on physicians of all kinds.

The second most important and uncertain stakeholder was the holding company. If you go with raising the price, then you have to assume, as the high-price group did, that the holding company is primarily interested in maximizing profits. That is, it will sell less of the drug (lower volume) but make more money per dose sold. On the other hand, if you lower the price, you have to assume, as the low-price group did, that the holding company is primarily interested in maximizing market-share. That is, you sell more of the drug (greater volume) but you make less money per dose sold. Neither one is necessarily wrong, they are merely different. Which one is best depends on the overall objectives of the parent *and* subsidiary drug company considered as a total *system.* Notice that although we started with just one part of the system, the drug company, we have ended up having to consider the whole system. This is in itself one of the prime features of complex problems. They involve or turn into a whole-systems problem.

If the assumption involving the holding company was so important, one might ask, "Why didn't the drug company merely call up or visit its 'parent' so close by?" The answer is, "If only organizational politics and jockeying for power, prestige, and influence were that simple!" Just to ask for clarification of something in some systems is not as simple as it may appear. Nor is it necessarily rewarded by those "on top" who may not know the answer and do not want to reveal their ignorance.

All the groups, on the other hand, felt that the patient wanted a low-cost quality product. Hence, all the groups placed their assumption regarding the patient in the upper right-hand quadrant.

We shall not bother to pursue here the further details of the methodology for resolving messy problems of this kind (see Mason and Mitroff, 1981). We shall merely note that all the executives were finally able as a result of this process to agree on one alternative to pursue. They decided to raise the price of the drug in certain key test locations and to monitor very carefully the reactions of critical stakeholders and, in this way, to test the validity of selective, crucial assumptions. If one lowers the price of the drug when one could have raised it, one will never find this out. On the other hand, if one raises it in certain test locations, one will find out very quickly if the market will support this action.

Note that one can still continue to disagree with the company's final action from a variety of other perspectives, one of which at some point would certainly be ethical. My point would still be that in either agreeing or disagreeing with the company one would be making some fundamental assumptions. There is no way to avoid making assumptions of some kind. Therefore, they need to be displayed and examined in such a way that they can be debated. As someone once said, "It is far better to debate a question without necessarily settling it than to settle a question without debating it." I would contend, not without debate of course, that more than ever we need tools that are appropriate to the kinds of complex problems we increasingly face.

Review of the Process

Let us review very briefly some of the key features of the process we have been examining. We started out by explaining that assumptions are rooted in the behavior of someone or some party. Assumptions, in short, pertain to stakeholders; they do not exist in a vacuum. The identification of stakeholders is a way of getting at assumptions. Most persons cannot readily name assumptions. They are too vague, too hazy, too hidden from view. Asking people to list the actors or parties involved or affected by one's actions, however, is concrete and do-able. Once stakeholders are identified, it is then relatively easy to ask, "What do I have to assume is true of a particular stakeholder so that starting from this assumption I can then derive or support my policy or my actions?"

Note that there is no guarantee that all groups will generate the same kinds of stakeholders as were named in the drug company case. This is thus one of the first ways in which groups can differ from one another. If they do, then they are making different assumptions about who is influencing or who ought to influence (at the very least be considered in) their situation. Many a group differs over "the basic right of recognition." As the modern corporation has grown it has had to consider more and more stakeholders than it did previously, whether it likes this or not. The same is now true of all organizations, public and private.

The second way in which groups can differ is in the qualitative form of the assumption or property they impute to a particular stakeholder. The physician in the drug company case is illustrative here. One group assumed price-insensitivity; the other assumed the opposite. Thus, the process helps to discover fundamental differences of this kind.

Third, groups can disagree over their importance and certainty rankings. Thus, for example, two groups could conceivably agree that the physician was a relevant stakeholder. Conceivably they could agree on the same qualitative assumption of price-insensitivity. However, one group could consider this to be very important and very uncertain to their policy, while the other could consider it to be very unimportant and very certain. The third step of mapping assumptions helps groups to see this. I want to emphasize the word *see* here because I believe strongly that often it is the failure to be able to observe assumptions that drives groups around in an endless circle. I have also deliberately emphasized each step in the process because the method, if

there really is just one, for working on complex problems *is
above all a behavioral process* for allowing persons to see their
differences in perceiving stakeholders (who is involved, who
should be considered), in naming assumptions (what the stakeholders are presumed to be like), and in mapping (what is important and what is felt to be known).

I often have the feeling that our differences of opinion
and perception are as much a result of the way we conduct ourselves as they are the result of truly conflicting ideas. We seem
to relish organizing ourselves into forms—usually circular ones—
that prevent us from airing and resolving our differences in anything resembling a constructive fashion. We just have to break
out of these circles.

Conclusion

This chapter has attempted to introduce a new way of
thinking about complex managerial and social systems. In effect, it has argued that social systems are constituted of stakeholders. It has also argued that we need new methods for systematically uncovering important stakeholders and their associated properties (assumptions) upon which an organization's
plans and actions depend. Again, I want to emphasize the key
word *systematically*. Many organizations pretend to follow the
method I am advocating, but they do not do the thorough, systematic job of monitoring stakeholders that is essential to suc-
ceeding with this approach. Little wonder that their policies
atrophy as the world pulls the rug out from under them.

Likewise, it is easy to identify four stances, really pathol-
ogies, toward planning that often develop in each of the four
cells in Figure 3. I have encountered groups that felt all their
assumptions fell into the unimportant, certain quadrant. This
group was saying in effect, "We know it all (everything is certain) but it does not matter (it is all unimportant)." Now, either
this group is right or they are playing a gigantic game of denying
reality or they are not risking anything new that would inevita-
bly get them into the uncertain cell. If you do something new,
then you cannot be completely certain.

Another common attitude is that nothing is known for

certain (it is all uncertain) but that it is all unimportant! In other words, "We know that we do not know but we also know that it does not matter!" This can be another defensive position. Again, I am talking about a situation in which all—or almost all—the assumptions a group makes fall into the unimportant and uncertain categories.

Another position still is to say that one knows it all and that it is all important. This attitude may be true or it may be empty arrogance. When every assumption falls into one cell, I tend to be very skeptical. So may others who listen to a group present such an assumption map.

Finally, there is the attitude that everything is important but uncertain. Groups oriented this way tend to feel overwhelmed by the world and may succumb to chaos.

Whenever an orientation is extreme, one-sided, the danger is that it will fail precisely where it has ignored the concerns that its counter-balancing opposites raise. This is why I advocate creating opposing perspectives on problems of critical importance to an organization. That is, if major differences do not already exist within the organization, as they did in the drug company, then they must be created by design to ensure that important dimensions of a problem will not be overlooked. Too much rides on today's decisions to pursue them from one and only one perspective, no matter who the advocate for any one single position may be. The most crucial thing we can do is to examine problems *systematically* from several different perspectives. Chapter Four shows how to do this by demonstrating one important basis for methodically creating different group perspectives, no matter what the problem. Diesing (1962) has put the matter well: "If one man knew the whole truth his predictions would always be correct; but since all existing theories [and approaches] are incomplete and partly false, it is better to bring together a variety of partial theories to better approximate the whole truth" (p. 179).

One of the major purposes of this book is to broaden our perspective of the forces (stakeholders and assumptions) which more than ever threaten to overwhelm us. To do this necessitates that we confront some of the most basic questions one can ever raise: "Where do stakeholders come from? Are there levels of stakeholders? Why? How are they organized? Is there a basic set of stakeholders? Is there a fundamental set of stakeholder properties? How, in short, do stakeholders influence our lives?" These are key points on the journey this book undertakes. The hope is that at the end we will have a better understanding of the wondrous and terrifying social world of which we are all a part, and which is stranger than anything we could design consciously and rationally.

CHAPTER THREE

External Influences on Managers

Stakeholders: The Constituent Elements of Purposeful Systems

One purpose of this chapter is to reveal a set of methods by which stakeholders can be generated at the institutional, organizational, political, and social levels of social system analysis. The other purpose is to show the kinds of properties associated with stakeholders and hence the kinds of assumptions that must be made about them.

The discussion in this and the preceding chapter follows from a rather complex view of social systems and a special philosophy of social science for understanding such systems. The best elaboration of this view can be found in the works of Ackoff and Emery (1974) and Churchman (1971, 1979). While it is difficult to capture the richness of their views, it is best attempted after we have examined some of the concrete properties of stakeholders. Before we do this, however, we shall discuss first several concrete methods for uncovering stakeholders.

Methods for Uncovering Stakeholders

There are no definite limits to the number of techniques that one could use to generate a set of stakeholders relevant to any given organizational problem. It must be kept in mind that we are dealing with complex, messy systems. As a result, we do not obtain the kind of closure and definitiveness that one does in simple, closed systems.

Seven methods have proved to be sufficient in stimulating the thinking of practitioners about the kinds of stakeholders inherent in the situations with which they must deal. The seven are imperative, positional, reputational, social participation, opinion-leadership, demographic, and organizational. Since each approach picks up stakeholders that the others miss, we (Mason and Mitroff, 1981) recommend that organizations use all of them in thinking about the forces in their environment.

The *imperative* approach identifies stakeholders who feel strongly enough about an organization's proposed policies or actions to act on their feelings. To use this method, one makes a list of as many as possible of the imperatives, slogans, and catchwords that have been uttered in the context of a policy issue. Also identified are any acts of defiance (for example, strikes, sit-ins, and lying in front of trucks) or other actions that suggest dissatisfaction with the policy system. The *sources* of the imperatives and acts are identified and each is considered as a potential stakeholder. The deficiency of this method is that it misses silent stakeholders who nevertheless may have a strong opinion on a policy issue.

Recent events painfully demonstrate the importance of using this method to think about one's organization. The placing of poisonous substances in the products of various drug companies reveals that the stakeholders that organizations must now deal with in their environment are no longer entirely benign. They include such evil characters as assassins, extorters, kidnappers, and saboteurs.

A fundamental point of this and the previous chapter is that while the pinpointing of such characters in one's particular organization can never be perfect or exact, it does not excuse organizations from thinking seriously about them and about what they can do to anticipate their vulnerable places. It does not follow that if one cannot have exact or perfect knowledge regarding every potential stakeholder, then one should not think about or anticipate them at all. This is precisely the attitude that must change if organizations are to survive in a more complex world. In today's world the systematic consideration of stakeholders might very well be a dire necessity and not a luxury.

The *positional* approach identifies those stakeholders that occupy formal positions in a policy-making structure, whether internal or external to the organization, for example, government. Organization charts and legal documents are a good source for this method. The deficiency of this approach is that it ignores important stakeholders that are not formally a part of the organization but have an impact on it nonetheless.

The *reputational* approach is a sociometric one. It entails asking various knowledgeable or important persons to nominate those whom they believe have a stake in the system. The deficiency here is that unorganized, nonelite, and disenfranchised groups may be ignored.

The *social-participation* approach identifies individuals or organizations as stakeholders to the extent that they participate in activities related to a policy issue. Membership in special organizations or committees, attendance at meetings, voting, and other instances of observable behavior are taken as evidence of having a potential stake in an issue. The obvious deficiency of this approach is that many latent, currently nonparticipatory stakeholders (for example, the silent majority, children, the aged, future generations) will be overlooked.

Since one of the reasons for identifying stakeholders is to assess their leverage and influence in a policy system, it is sometimes adequate to identify only those who tend to shape the opinions of other stakeholders. The *opinion-leadership* method does this. Examples would be the editors of important magazines, newspapers, and journals. This approach has the advantage of identifying important stakeholders who are not part of the formal structure or do not have the same status as those selected by previous methods. Its disadvantage is that it is less precise and requires more judgment on the part of the analyst than do some of the other methods.

The *demographic* approach identifies stakeholders by such characteristics as age, sex, race, occupation, religion, place of birth, and level of education. For many policy, planning, and strategy issues, these distinctions are necessary, since it is to be expected that a policy will have a different impact on different demographic groups. The disadvantage of this approach is that it assumes homogeneity of interest within any particular group.

The last method selects a *focal organization* (for example, the drug company in Chapter Two) in a policy system and seeks to identify the individuals and organizations who have important relationships with the focal organization. Typical relationships are those of (1) supplier, (2) employee, (3) customer or client, (4) ally, (5) competitor or adversary, (6) regulator or controller (for example, government), and (7) regulatee or controlee (for example, subdivisions of a parent organization, legally controlled entities). (Again, see the drug company example in the preceding chapter.) The advantage of this approach is that it identifies potential parties or elements that other approaches can overlook. It has the disadvantage of not being comprehensive and of potentially missing some key stakeholders such as opinion leaders.

Stakeholder Assumptions

For ease of presentation, stakeholder properties may be subdivided into two categories: intrinsic and extrinsic. Intrinsic properties are those that may be defined independent of other stakeholders. Extrinsic properties are those that arise as a result of the interaction and relationships with other stakeholders. Extrinsic properties become especially important when one stakeholder attempts to change another. As we shall see, it is easier to state the difference between intrinsic and extrinsic properties than it is to keep them strictly apart.

My view of stakeholders and their associated properties may be summarized in a number of key propositions:

1. An organization or social system is an organized collection of internal and external stakeholders. This is not as trivial as it may appear. The word *organized* implies that at least one critical property of a stakeholder will be influenced by

the property of at least one other stakeholder. Assumptions naturally come into play because parties will differ as to which stakeholder influences which other. The drug company case in Chapter Two is an example of this.

2. Each stakeholder is a distinct and distinguishable entity that has resources, purposes, and a will of its own. Thus it is capable of volitional or purposeful behavior (Ackoff and Emery, 1974). The detailed kinds of properties that characterize a stakeholder's behavior may be subdivided as follows. Note that each stakeholder has at least one important property in at least one of the following categories:

    a. The purposes and motivations of a stakeholder.

    b. The beliefs that a stakeholder has or that can be ascribed to it.

    c. The resources a stakeholder commands; among these are

        (1) Material resources.

        (2) Symbolic resources (for example, those pertaining to political office).

        (3) Physical resources.

        (4) Positional resources (for example, privileged position in a social or informational network).

        (5) Informational resources (for example, access to special or privileged sources).

        (6) Skill.

    d. Special knowledge and opinions.

    e. Commitments, legal and otherwise.

    f. Relationships to other stakeholders in the system by virtue of

        (1) Power.

        (2) Authority.

        (3) Responsibility.

        (4) Accountability.

Disagreements among the proponents of different policies usually occur because they typically ascribe or impute very different properties to the same set of stakeholders. For instance, in the drug company case the proponents of the three policies disagreed across almost every one of the six

categories listed earlier that characterize stakeholder properties. They ascribed different purposes and motivations to
almost all of the stakeholders in their case; they imputed
different beliefs to them; they perceived the resources of
each stakeholder differently; and so forth.

3. There is a network of interdependent *relationships* among
all stakeholders. Some relationships are *supporting* in that
they provide movement toward the organization's purposes.
Some relationships are *resisting* in that they serve as barriers or encourage movement away from the organization's
purposes. (See the properties listed earlier under item 2f.)
This is the minimal sense in which an organization or social
system is an organized collection of stakeholders.

4. A new strategy, that is, a change in strategy for an organization, changes one or more of the relationships among the
stakeholders. Hence, every action is dependent on stakeholder properties and vice versa.

5. Relationships with each stakeholder (that is, stakeholder
properties) may be changed in one or more of the following
ways. Note that whether a stakeholder is susceptible to a
particular means of change is itself an additional property
of a stakeholder:

  a. Convert (change) the stakeholder by means of:

    (1) Commanding him or her through the exercise
    of power and authority.

    (2) Persuading him or her by appealing to rea-
    son, values, and emotion.

    (3) Bargaining with him or her by means of eco-
    nomic exchange.

    (4) Negotiating with him or her to reach "give
    and take" compromises.

    (5) Problem solving with him or her by means
    of sharing, debating, and arriving at agreed
    upon mutual perceptions.

  b. Fight the stakeholder and politic to overpower him
  or her by means of:

    (1) Securing and marshalling the organization's
    resources.

    (2) Forming coalitions with other stakeholders.

   (3)   Destroying the stakeholder.

c.   Absorb aspects of a stakeholder's demands by incor-
     porating them by means of co-optation.
d.   Coalesce with the stakeholder by forming a coalition
     with joint decision-making powers.
e.   Avoid or ignore the stakeholder.
f.   Appease the stakeholder by giving in to some of his
     or her demands.
g.   Surrender to the stakeholder.
h.   Love the stakeholder by forming an intense emo-
     tional bond or special relationship with him or her.
i.   Be or become the stakeholder by transforming the
     organization into the stakeholder through merger,
     imitation, idolatry, or role modeling.

Any strategy must be implemented through one or more of
these ways of affecting change. Hence, all strategies presuppose power, that is, the ability to employ a relevant set of
methods for bringing about change. Little wonder, having
identified these different ways of changing stakeholders,
that analysts of a social system and policy makers often advocate such different policies. All of the properties regarding stakeholders and their ability to change through a certain
means are highly volatile, changing, and subject to debate.
It is exceedingly easy to assume very different capabilities
with regard to each stakeholder's ability to change.

6.   The state of an organization at a certain point in time will
     be the result of the interaction of the behavior of all the or-
     ganization's stakeholders from the beginning of its history
     up to a particular point in time. This extended history may
     be referred to as the "culture" of the organization or of the
     extended set of stakeholders.

7.   A strategy undertaken at one point in time to achieve out-
     comes at a later point *must* be based on one or more *as-
     sumptions* about (a) the properties and behavior of the
     stakeholders, (b) the network of relationships that binds
     them to the organization, and (c) the organization's power
     to change relevant relationships. Assumptions must be
     made because (a), (b), and (c) taken by themselves, or even

collectively, are too complex for any person (that is, stakeholder) to have complete, perfect, or certain knowledge
about them.

A Further Word About Purposeful Systems

As mentioned earlier, everything in this chapter follows
from a special view of social systems. This view is neither easy
to state nor to summarize. One way to approach it is to discuss
the functions necessary to the existence and maintenance of social systems. Philosophers of science such as Ackoff, Churchman, and Singer have proposed four such functions:

1. The ability to change purposes (ends) and to create new
   purposes. Ackoff, Churchman, and Singer call this the
   Aesthetic Dimension. By aesthetic they mean something
   more than the traditional concept of aesthetics—the pursuit
   and meaning of the Beautiful. As I construe it, this may be
   conceived of as the Creativity and Change Dimension. In
   this sense, aesthetics refers to the characteristic style of an
   organization. It also refers to the organization's sense of
   quality, that is, what it instinctively feels is worth pursuing.
2. The ability to acquire and mobilize adequate resources
   (means). This can be referred to as the Political and Economic Dimension, for politics and economics in their
   broadest possible senses pertain to the effective acquisition
   and use of means.
3. The ability to discover and develop resources and to allocate the right resource in the right amounts to the right organizational component at the right time, that is, the ability to relate means to ends effectively. This dimension obviously relates to the proper use of knowledge and information. Thus, this is naturally referred to as the Information
   and Communication Dimension.
4. The ability to sustain cooperation and to eliminate conflict
   among all stakeholders so that basic purposes are achiev-
   able. This is referred to as the Ethical, Moral, Cooperative
   Dimension.

Each of these broad dimensions could be expanded indefinitely. Richard Mason and I have recently attempted to do this by showing some of the conditions that would have to be met to obtain each of the functions of Ackoff, Churchman, and Singer. Following each condition we have placed in parentheses some of the many key areas and concepts from the field of management and organizational sciences that would have to be considered in order to attain that condition. The concepts thus show the tremendous complexity and interdisciplinary nature of the task involved in attaining each condition. Note that the conditions have been deliberately worded in the ideal. As a result, they help to draw out even further the nature of the tremendous assumptions that must be made if an organization is to perform satisfactorily or even exist.

1. Change and Creativity.
    a. The leaders of the organization must have the inspiration and creativity necessary to reevaluate the organization's current missions, purposes, objectives, and goals and to conceptualize new purposes. (Leadership, Statesmanship, Goal-Setting, Missions, Management by Objectives.)
    b. The managers must have the capability for translating new concepts, ideas, and purposes into concrete, visualizable programs of action. (Innovation, Creativity, Management of Change, Organizational Change, Invention, Protection of Change through Patents and Copyrights, Flexibility, Changeability.)
    c. All stakeholders must have the spirit, dedication, and commitment necessary to secure new purposes. (Motivation, Incentives, Satisfaction, Promotions, Careers, Personal Values, Organizational and Individual Renewal, Burnout, Catharsis, Energy, Drive.)
2. Business—Political and Economic Functions.
    a. The total resources held by the collection of stakeholders must be adequate to accomplish their purposes. (Capital Availability, Recruitment, Capital Budgeting, Finance, Purchasing, Energy, Mergers,

Acquisition, Plant Location, Working Capital, Cash Flow, Inventory, Dividend Policy.)

b. The managers must reallocate the resources from stakeholder to stakeholder so that each stakeholder possesses the amount of resources necessary to carry out its tasks at the right time and place. (Budgeting, Decision Making, Resource Allocation.)

c. The stakeholders must employ the resources they have effectively and efficiently when executing their tasks to ensure that maximally useful output is produced. (Productivity, Production, Job Assignment, Organization Structure, Materials Handling, Design of Jobs.)

d. The managers must distribute the output effectively to all relevant stakeholders. (Marketing, Sales, Distribution, Sales Force, Sales Training, Advertising, Customer Relations.)

3. Information and Communication.

a. The collection of stakeholders must have the capacity to acquire or produce basic knowledge—scientific, industrial, and operations—about the organization's products, technology, operations, finances, markets, and customers. (R and D, Accounting, Management Information Systems, Market Research, Operations Research, Corporate Intelligence, Planning, Library.)

b. The managers must ensure that the right information is transmitted to the right stakeholder at the right time. (Communications, Organization, Reporting, Dissemination, Education, Training, Advertising, Public Affairs, Auditing, Storage and Retrieval, Telecommunications, Teleconferencing.)

c. Each stakeholder must have the capacity to use the knowledge and information he or she receives to make effective decisions. (Management Systems, Knowledge Utilization, Applied Research, Participation, Boards of Directors, Policy-Making Structure, Authority, Responsibility, Accountability, Cognitive Style, Intuitive Decision Making, Decision Processes.)

4. Ethical, Moral, Cooperative.
    a. Stakeholders must have the necessary peace of mind
        within themselves to be effective in their organiza-
        tional life and the other aspects of their life. (Mid-
        Life Crisis, Quality of Work Life, Human Potential
        Movement, Satisfaction, Health and Safety, Stabil-
        ity, Fringe Benefits, Stress, Psychic Energy.)
    b. There must be a minimum of conflict between the
        internal stakeholders—individuals, groups, depart-
        ments—that function within the organization. (Or-
        ganization Development, Role Clarification, Conflict
        Resolution, Leadership, Dissention, Goldbricking.)
    c. There must be a minimum of conflict between the
        organization and its external stakeholders such as
        governments, public interest groups, social activists,
        unions, and competitors. (Public Relations, Govern-
        ment Relations, Labor Relations, Ethics, Morality,
        Social Responsibility, Product Safety SEC, EPA,
        EEOC, OSHA, OPEC, Issues Management, Freedom
        of Information, Anti-Trust.)

Stakeholders and Rationality

Nothing that has been said in this chapter is meant to imply that the four functions that I have borrowed from Ackoff,
Churchman, and Singer are necessarily unique to them. In a profound and undeservedly neglected book, *Reason in Society,*
Diesing (1962) identifies four basic types of rationality or functions that he argues are fundamental to a complex society.
These are economic, political, legal, and social rationality. While
different on the surface, Diesing's four types of rationality or
social system functions are, for all practical purposes, identical
to the four discussed earlier. What is important is not the particular names of the functions but that Diesing gives independent
support for the existence of the distinct kinds of functions necessary to the operation of complex social systems. Even more
important, Diesing is able to show that none of the functions is
really able to exist without some *minimal* existence of the oth-

ers. For instance, consider what Diesing terms economic rationality. In the ideal, economic rationality is based on the notion of economic *order*. Economic order exists when there is a universally recognized system of measurement (for example, dollars) such that different things and commodities can be compared in terms of their value with regard to the accepted units of measurement. There must be some minimal social rationality or solidarity within the members of a social system for a *common* system of measurement to be recognized and accepted as universally valid. Thus, all of the functions are *interdependent* in some basic sense. None can exist or function without the others.

An important implication emerges from this insight. No single stakeholder has a complete or totally separate existence of its own. In a complex social system, each stakeholder is tied to or dependent upon *at least one other* important social system stakeholder for its existence and/or functioning. This implies that *the properties of each stakeholder are dependent upon or a function of the properties of at least one other stakeholder in the entire system of stakeholders*. Put somewhat differently, *the assumptions that are made about the behavior of each stakeholder are a function of the assumptions made about the behavior of at least one other stakeholder in the system. Thus, every intrinsic property of a stakeholder is influenced by an extrinsic property of at least one other stakeholder.* We are truly dealing with a network or a system of behavior.

The preceding point establishes one of the most important properties of stakeholders at the level of social system analysis. It does not, however, establish all of them. Actually, a number of other principles were stated implicitly in Chapter Two. One such principle holds that, since some assumptions are judged to be more important and certain than others, *stakeholders can be ranked hierarchically according to their importance and the confidence one has in determining their properties.*

The most important property of stakeholders at this level is the *presumption* of rationality. In its most basic sense, this means that stakeholders cannot possess contradictory properties. A stakeholder cannot be strong and weak, rich and poor, at the same time. This might seem to contradict the discussion in

Chapter Two of the physician who was imputed to be both price-sensitive and price-insensitive. The key word, however, is *imputed*. The physician was *perceived by* different groups to be different things. Presumably, though, a given physician could not be both at the same time, nor could a *single* group perceive a given physician to be both price-insensitive and price-sensitive.

There presumably exists an objective way, or ways, of settling the dispute.

These beliefs make for a rational conception of stakeholders. Indeed, most of what currently passes for organization theory, social systems analyses, sociology, and political science adheres to the presumption of rationality. With few exceptions the overwhelming emphasis is on the disinterested, impersonal, supposedly rational analysis of stakeholders. This mode of thinking can take the following form: "*If* stakeholder X has properties p, q, and so on, *then* X can cause stakeholder Y to behave in such-and-such a way." The discovery of such if-then relationships or impersonal laws is the overriding aim of the vast bulk of what we know as contemporary social science. As such, its aim is to emulate the physical sciences.

What is wrong with this? Nothing—when it is taken in its proper perspective (see Chapter Eight). But when it extends outside its proper domain of meaning, it gives us an incomplete and distorted picture of the complexities of human behavior. It is vitally important to appreciate that the theory of stakeholders presented thus far holds only for *surface* social system stakeholders, that is, those stakeholders conceived of as rational, calculating devices. It does not hold for stakeholders endowed with highly complex, emotional makeups. To treat this emotionality—even to acknowledge it—necessitates that we penetrate beneath the surface of stakeholders rationally conceived and rationally endowed.

To illustrate my point, consider the fact that in all the times my colleagues and I have applied the method of assumptions analysis, we have never encountered a case wherein any in-depth, sophisticated attribution or treatment of stakeholder properties was achieved. This does not mean that the users of the method did not achieve important insights, for they did.

This surface level treatment of stakeholders is not particularly surprising. The participants have been, for the most part, lay social system analysts, not professional social scientists. Even the social scientists rarely penetrate beneath the surface of things to offer a "deep structure" theory of human motivations.

My colleagues and I have tried to aid and even to push participants into thinking more deeply about a wider class of stakeholders and a deeper set of properties. For instance, we have encouraged participants to think about nonobvious stakeholders. We call them *snaildarters* after the endangered species of fish that held up a proposed hydroelectric project for years. In all their rational plans the designers of the dam had failed to take the snaildarter into account. As a result, one class of stakeholders, environmentalists, acted in behalf of another stakeholder, the snaildarter, that could not act in its own behalf.

The lesson of the snaildarter is paramount. Just beneath the surface of the best laid and most rational plans swim forces of which people are entirely unaware and do not wish to consider. These seemingly tiny and insignificant forces, however, have a strange way of wrecking the most well-conceived plans and policies.

This chapter began by revealing some rather straightforward ways to generate and to analyze stakeholders at the surface level of social systems. Step by step we have been led to the need for digging deeper into the concept of stakeholders. Are there classes of stakeholders that lie beneath the surface of those stakeholders that are most visible? If so, what are they? How do these less visible stakeholders influence those that we can see? As we shall see, in the answers to these questions lies a deeper, more complex psychoanalytic theory for managing complex social systems. It is, however, as was mentioned in the preface to this book, a psychoanalytic theory in a nontraditional sense. Although guided by the immense insights of such giants as Freud and Jung, it attempts to formulate them in ways more accessible and relevant to those charged with managing the ever-widening disarray of things.

Finally, I would be the first to acknowledge that there is a certain unsatisfying incompleteness to our discussion thus far, particularly in this chapter, which displays an all-too-common malaise in the social sciences: It is a laundry list of concerns and issues. I have despairingly referred to it as a "philosophy of lists."

Such lists are unfortunately due to the basic character of the phenomena we are dealing with. For one, the number of stakeholders one must deal with in complex systems is so large, so varied, and so quickly changing that it would be almost impossible to create with any confidence a single, unchanging, timeless theory for describing the behavior of all stakeholders and their impacts on one another for any extended period of time.

One can still have a general social science with special emphasis on the word *science*. But a different kind of social "science" is needed to deal with the changing, uncertain nature of stakeholders and their associated properties. The general features of this social science were outlined in the preceding chapter (see also Mason and Mitroff, 1981; and Mitroff and Kilmann, 1978). One of the basic purposes of such a social science is precisely to allow those with different perceptions to debate whether a certain stakeholder has a certain set of properties and whether a certain stakeholder influences other stakeholders. That is, it is more important to have a method whereby the members of an organization facing a particular problem can work the lists of stakeholders than to present a single list of stakeholders that holds for all organizations and their problems.

Even if we were to consider whether all of the properties of stakeholders in one category were in theory derivable from another, we would not really be out of a dilemma. For instance, suppose that one were a Marxist social scientist. As a result, suppose that one insisted that all of, say, what Diesing labels as legal, political, and social rationality were derived solely from economic conditions. Suppose, too, that one contended that legal, political, and social behavior were solely or primarily a function of the economic modes of production of a society. Now, there is nothing inherently wrong with this argument per se, except to say that it is an assumption. Not only is this assumption not accepted by all social analysts or stakeholders themselves but, more crucial still, it is an assumption that, although vitally important, is no more certain than many of the other assumptions that describe a complex social system.

The somewhat inevitable laundry-list character of our social science demonstrates the particular kinds of complexities that a social science of complex problems faces. The question that confronts us is whether this complexity will become even greater or paradoxically less as we discover the even greater complexity of stakeholders. That is, will recognizing the even greater complexity of stakeholders lead to a greater or less complex way of thinking about social systems? If elegance of social theory escapes us at the level of this chapter, may it nonetheless be found later in this volume, after we have seen the enormously greater complexity of human life? Finally, if the elegance of social science is not necessarily to be found in its formal theories about the substance of social systems, can it thereby be found in the sophistication of its methods for investigating incredibly changing phenomena? If the essence of humanity is indeed truly invention, then let us invent a method that measures up to the phenomenon that is humanity.

CHAPTER FOUR

The Manager's Personality
as Stakeholder

Any theory of psychotherapy is essentially a set of assumptions. Whether explicit or implicit, these assumptions dictate the therapist's approach with patients [Gentry, 1981, p. 111].

In the next two chapters we begin examination of those stakeholders or stakeholder influences that lie beneath the surface of ordinary life. I attempt to show that the human psyche may be construed as a particular kind of miniature social system. If an organization or a social system may be construed as a collection of a particular set of stakeholders, then the individual human psyche may be construed as a collection of a different set of stakeholders. In a word, if Chapters Two and Three have examined those stakeholders that operate at the level of collective social life—the social system—then this chapter begins examination of those kinds of stakeholders and influences that

Note: Many ideas and data reported in this chapter derive from "Stories Managers Tell: A New Tool for Organizational Problem Solving" by I. Mitroff and R. Kilmann. Portions reprinted, by permission of the publisher, from *Management Review*, July 1975, © 1975 by AMACOM, a division of American Management Associations, New York. All rights reserved.

operate at the level beneath the social system—the individual personality and psyche. It is the peculiar kinds of interactions among stakeholders at these two levels of social reality—the social system and the individual—that lead to a psychoanalytically based or, more precisely, psychosocial theory of human systems.

We begin our discussion with a treatment of individual personality differences relevant to the management of human systems. Imagine that, like the chief executive officer of the drug company in Chapter Two, you are the head of an organization, public or private. Imagine further that for whatever reasons you are also interested in learning how you and your executive staff typically approach problems. As a result, you arrange to hold a special kind of offsite workshop.

The workshop begins with the administration of a short personality instrument designed to measure a person's cognitive style. The instrument is primarily designed and used to measure how people construe their reality and orient themselves to the world. Its primary intent is not to diagnose personality disorders, although it can be used for that purpose.

The workshop leaders (my colleagues and I have actually conducted these kinds of workshops) explain that their use of the instrument is merely to assist the participants in helping them discover how they look at the world. After the participants have taken the instrument and self-scored it (which typically takes about ten to fifteen minutes), they are placed into various groups based on their scores. All those who share the same personality profile, as measured by the instrument, are, as much as is possible, placed into a common group. As a result of this procedure, a group of twenty or so participants is sorted into four to five subgroupings. The participants are instructed that the instrument and the basis for how they were grouped will be explained to them later. Explaining both at this point would merely defeat the purpose and the fun of the exercise.

Next, depending on the group and the purposes to be accomplished, each subgroup is given either a standard Tinkertoy set, a common set of pictures cut out from a series of magazines, or a blank tablet. If they are given a Tinkertoy set, they are asked to build a "construction" which "best represents their subgroup's idea of 'society's most important problem.' " If they are given a set of magazine pictures, they are asked to use the pictures in any manner they wish to tell a story—any story they wish—that "links together the pictures in any way they see fit." If they are given a blank tablet, they are asked to write a "story that best expresses their idea of their 'ideal organization.' "

One of the basic purposes of all three assignments is to make personality, an internal state or disposition which by definition is almost impossible "to see," externally visible. Since each subgroup is constructed as much as possible to be homogeneous, it projects its common personality disposition onto the task. As a result, the exercises help make visible the inordinately complex phenomenon of personality. In my opinion this is the fundamental meaning of the rather foreboding term *phenomenology*. It means or should mean nothing more than "making visible how humans construe phenomena."

I can illustrate the outcome of these exercises by discussing the one especially germane to this book: different persons' concept of their ideal organization. As a general rule, my colleagues and I have found that there are four basic forms or types of ideal organizations that emerge from this exercise.

The Ideal Organizations of Type Ones

The stories of the first type of ideal organization typically contain an extreme emphasis and concentration on specifics, on factual details. Type One managers are extremely sensitive to the physical features of their work environment. For example, the stories of Type Ones display an extreme preoccupation with environments that are neither "too hot" nor "too cold" but "just right." The ideal organization of Type Ones is characterized by complete control, certainty, and specificity. In their ideal organization, everybody knows *exactly* what his or her job is. There is no uncertainty or ambiguity whatsoever as to what is expected in any circumstance. Furthermore, Type One organizations are impersonal. The emphasis is on work and work roles, not on the particular individuals who fill the roles. The ideal organization of Type Ones is authoritarian, perhaps the very epitome of bureaucracy. There is a single leader at the top and a well-defined hierarchical line of authority that extends from the very top down to all of the lower rungs of the organization. In a Type One organization, the individuals exist to serve the goals of the organization, not the organization to serve the goals of the individuals.

The goals of a Type One organization are realistic, down-to-earth, limited in their scope and time horizon, and, more often than not, narrowly economic. That is, they are concerned with precise measures of output to input or technical efficiency. For these reasons, Type One organizations can be termed internal-technical. Their focus is turned inward and oriented toward technical concerns.

Finally, the heroes or leaders of Type Ones are tough-minded individuals who know how "to step on people to get the job done." The greatest achievement of the heroes of Type Ones is that they were available when the firm needed what they had to offer most: They brought "order and stability out of chaos; they gave the organization a specific, well-defined sense of direction."

The Ideal Organizations of Type Twos

The stories of Type Twos are marked by an extreme emphasis on broad, global issues. In describing their ideal organization, Type Twos do not specify the detailed work rules, roles, or lines of authority but focus instead on general concepts and issues. Thus if the organizational goals of Type Ones are concerned with well-defined, precise microeconomic issues—"We need to make X dollars by September 13 to stay solvent"—then the goals of Type Twos are concerned with broader, less well-defined or precise macroeconomic issues—"There ought to be an equitable wage for all workers," or, "We ought to be monitoring the environment for new opportunities as well as threats." Like Type One organizations, Type Two organizations are impersonal. However, where Type Ones focus on the *details* of a specific impersonal organization, Type Twos focus on impersonal concepts and *global* theories of organization. For example, they are concerned with concepts of efficiency in the abstract. Likewise, whereas individuals in a Type One organization exist to serve the present and specific needs of their particular organization, individuals in a Type Two organization exist to serve the intellectual and theoretical concepts of the organization in general. In a word, if Type One organizations are impersonally *realistic,* then Type Two organizations are impersonally *idealistic.*

The heroes of Type Twos are broad conceptualizers. If the heroes of Type Ones are problem solvers, then the heroes of Type Twos are problem formulators, that is, the finders and the creators of new problems and challenges. The heroes of Type Twos take an organization designed to accomplish a very specific, limited set of goals (for example, turning out a specific product) and create broad new goals. They envision new products, new markets, long-term time horizons, and new businesses for their firm.

In the organization theory literature, the ideal organizations of Type Twos are termed matrix. Roles, jobs, rewards, and authority systems are more broadly defined than in the ideal Type One organization. This is because of the flexibility and adaptive character of ideal Type Two organizations. Groups must be freer to organize and reorganize if they are to respond effectively to constantly shifting and developing new external markets. That is, people are not assigned to fixed tasks and to fixed groups but rotate in and out of both as the need arises.

Type Two organizations may also be termed R and D (Research and Development) organizations since the emphasis is on the discovery, invention, and production of new technologies. They are constantly seeking new ideas to anticipate and create new external markets, not merely to respond to them. The primary measure of performance is the number of new ideas produced in the form of inventions, patents, and so on. For this reason, it is no exaggeration to say that their primary orientation is external-technical or macroeconomic; external in the sense that they are oriented toward the external environment and technical in the senses I have just described.

Since both Type Ones and Type Twos share an impersonal orientation, their stories are not stories in the true sense (see Chapter Eight). They read more like lists of characteristics or abstract descriptions. As a result, their "stories" read like the examples given in this and the preceding section.

The Ideal Organizations of Type Threes

The stories of Type Threes, like Type Twos, are marked by an extreme preoccupation with broad, global themes and issues and an extreme disdain toward getting down to specifics. However, Type Threes differ from Type Twos in that where the emphasis of Type Twos is on the general theory or *theoretical* aspects of organizations, the emphasis of Type Threes is on the most general *personal* and *human* goals of organizations. Thus Type Three organizations are concerned with "serving humanity," with "making a contribution to humanity." Type Threes differ from both Type Ones and Type Twos in that for the latter the individual exists to serve the organization, whereas for Type Threes the organization exists to serve the personal and social needs of people.

Since, in the personality theory underlying the instrument used to sort the participants into the different subgroups, the Type Three is the extreme opposite of the Type One, it is not surprising to find that the ideal organization of Type Threes is the exact opposite of the ideal of Type Ones. Thus, if a Type One organization is authoritarian and bureaucratic with extremely well-defined rules of behavior, then a Type Three organization is completely decentralized with no clear lines of authority, no central leader, and no fixed, prescribed rules of behavior. The stories of Type Threes often include the concepts of "flexibility" and "decentralization." As a matter of fact, many of the stories of Type Threes contain diagrams showing their ideal organization to be circular or wheel-like in structure rather than hierarchical. Indeed, the "stories" of Type Threes are more often than not no more than a diagram with very few words. Everyone is free to talk and to interact with everyone else without fear of exceeding one's authority or station. Type Three organizations are also idealistic as opposed to realistic. In essence, Type Three organizations are the epitome of organic, adaptive institutions, as they are known in the organization theory literature. They could be called external-people organizations. They are oriented both to the long-term, external environment and to people.

The heroes of Type Threes are not only able to envision new lines of direction, that is, new goals, objectives, and so forth, for their organization—in this sense they are like the heroes of Type Twos—but they are also able to give the organization a new sense of direction in the human or personal sense.

The Ideal Organizations of Type Fours

The ideal organizations of Type Twos and Type Fours are extreme opposites. If Type Twos are concerned with the general theory of all organizations but not with the details of any particular organization, then the Type Fours do not care at all about theory or issues in general. Type Fours are concerned instead with the detailed human relations in their particular organization. Type Fours are like Type Ones in that they are concerned with details and facts. However, Type Fours differ from Type Ones in that the latter are concerned with impersonal, detailed *work rules* and *roles* whereas the former are concerned with the *human qualities of the specific people* who fill the roles. Type Fours are, in this sense, similar to Type Threes in that both are concerned with the *people* in the organization. Type Fours differ from Type Threes in the sense that where Type Threes are concerned with people in general, Type Fours are concerned with individuals in particular. Type Threes are typically concerned with humanity as a whole, Type Fours with their immediate family and close friends.

Type Four organizations are realistic as opposed to idealistic. Like Type Ones, Type Fours are concerned with the detailed work environment although, where for Type Ones the environment of concern is physical, for Type Fours it is the interpersonal environment that is of concern. The heroes of Type Fours are those very special people who are able to create a highly personal, very warm human climate in their organization. They make you want to come to work. Indeed, the organization becomes just like home, like a family. For these reasons, they could well be termed internal-people organizations.

Only the Type Fours come closest to producing what one would truly call a "story." For that reason, I have included an example only from a Type Four:

Utopia in the Business World

The day had been a particularly harrowing one at the office with more than the normal amount of frustrations with the administration, the workers, and even the public. I went home and fell exhausted into bed.

Suddenly I awoke and looked around. Where was I? What was this strange place? Who were these people? At that moment I was approached by a smiling person with hand extended who said, "Welcome to our organization. We are glad to have you with us. My name is _____. I will take you around to meet the rest of the staff."

Everyone I met was very friendly and in the days to come proved to be most helpful. My duties were explained to me quite clearly and thoroughly. The procedure with which I had to work was written in such a way that there was very little chance of misinterpretation.

All of the staff worked quite well with each other with a minimum of disagreements. The separate department heads would meet once a week with the administrator who would keep them informed of new developments. The department heads would then keep the workers informed. Once a month the administrator would address the entire staff. There was a free and easy exchange of ideas. There was no CIA atmosphere nor were there always a lot of rumors floating around. No one ever said, "I heard by the grapevine." There was no need to hear by the grapevine. Everyone was fully informed as to the opportunities available to them.

A door slammed and suddenly I was transported from the ideal organization back to the world from which I came [Mitroff and Kilmann, 1975].

Behind the Stories

Now that the various types of ideal organizations have been presented, we can ask what lies behind the differences. Obviously, personality differences do since that is the basis on which the groups were constructed. However, another factor is the task itself. Like the Tinkertoy or magazine exercises, making up a story about one's ideal organization is inherently a projective device. Since there is no one right or wrong answer to the task, as the different stories clearly reveal, the response one gives is obviously a result of one's internal personality or disposition. Finally, another factor is the subgroups themselves. Putting like types or styles together reinforces and intensifies a particular way of looking at the world.

The personality framework behind the instrument used to sort the managers, or participants, is based on the pioneering work of Carl Jung. The Jungian structure was chosen for two main reasons: (1) the dimensions of the framework are directly related to different managerial and organizational styles, hence the classifications are of direct relevance to management and (2) the Jungian framework does not prescribe any one of its four major personality types as being superior to any of the others. Instead, each type is seen as having major strengths and weaknesses. The framework can help managers see that their personal style has certain costs or limitations as well as benefits and that, as a result, they need their managerial counterparts with markedly different personal styles to compensate for their weaknesses—and vice versa.

Two dimensions of the Jungian framework are of particular importance. The first dimension corresponds to the way in which a manager typically takes in data from the outside world. This is the *input-data dimension*. The second dimension corresponds to the way in which a manager typically makes a decision based on the data. This is the *decision-making dimension*.

According to Jung, individuals can take in data from the outside world by either *sensation* or *intuition*; most individuals tend to use one kind of data-input process rather than the other. Sensing, or sensation, "types" typically take in information via their senses. Sensing types are most comfortable when attending to the details, the specifics, of any situation. That is, sensing types tend to break every situation down into isolated bits and pieces; furthermore, they feel most comfortable when they have gathered some hard facts that pertain to the situation. In contrast, intuitive types typically take in information by looking at the situation as a whole. They concentrate their attention on the hypothetical possibilities in a situation rather than getting bogged down and constrained by details and an endless array of hard facts. All individuals perceive the world with both functions at different times. But, as Jung repeatedly argued, individuals tend to develop a habitual way of perceiving a situation and, in fact, cannot apply both types of perceiving or data input at the same time.

To appreciate the significance of this, it is important to realize that different types not only take in different kinds of data from the world but they typically recognize different things as data. That is, different types take in different things which they then call data or information because they have different internal standards or filters of legitimacy. What an opposing style or type calls data is not necessarily data for another.

Jung also posited that there are two basic ways of reaching a decision with regard to any situation: *thinking* and *feeling*. Thinking types base their decisions on impersonal, logical modes of reasoning. That is, thinking types do not feel comfortable unless they have a logical or an analytical (for example, mathematical) basis for making a decision. Feeling types, however, make their decisions based on personal considerations, for example, how they *feel* about the particular person or situation, whether they *like* the person or *value* the situation, and so forth. Thinking types, on the one hand, want to depersonalize every situation, object, and person by "explaining" them and having rules for correct conduct. Feeling types, on the other hand, want to personalize every situation, object, and person by stressing its individual uniqueness. Neither type is necessarily any better or more correct, merely different.

Thinking is the psychological function that generalizes; feeling, the function that individuates. Thinking takes two objects that are inherently dissimilar and seeks to find what they have in common. Feeling takes two objects, people, or situations that are inherently alike and emphasizes or seeks to find what is distinctly dissimilar about them. In short, thinking emphasizes sameness; feeling, characteristic differences or uniqueness, for example, that no two people are exactly alike.

In summary, however an individual takes in data, either

by intuition or sensation, he or she may come to some conclusion about the data either by a logical, impersonal analysis—thinking—or by a subjective, personal process—feeling.

Combining the two data-input modes—sensation and intuition—with the two decision-making modes—feeling and thinking—in all possible ways allows us to talk about the following four Jungian personality types:

- Sensing-thinking types (STs)
- Sensing-feeling types (SFs)
- Intuition-thinking types (NTs)
- Intuition-feeling types (NFs)

Readers can test how well they understand the Jungian framework by seeing if they can match the correct Jungian type with the stories presented earlier. Thus, the ideal organization of the ST is that of Type One; NT, Type Two; NF, Type Three; and SF, Type Four (see Figure 4).

Very rarely have I observed that this kind of exercise has

Figure 4. The Four Ideal Organizations and the Jungian Dimensions.

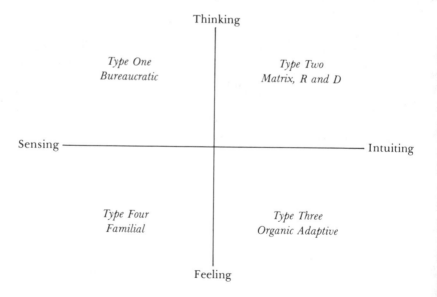

not had a powerful effect on the participants. Who among us does not relish learning something about oneself and others? Who among us does not relish learning why others mean something totally different by what are supposedly the same words, for example, "ideal organization"? The point is that when it comes to the individuality of the human psyche, there are no totally neutral words or concepts. To illustrate how deep the differences we are talking about extend, Feeling would contend that there are no totally neutral words; Thinking would contend that there are some words that are neutral.

The power of this deceptively simple exercise extends even further. It provides an interesting link between individual and societal behavior. Although Jung developed his theory of personality to explain differences among individuals, the exercise shows how the Jungian framework can be used to shed insight on organizational and institutional differences. That is, from one perspective, differences in organizational forms or types can be seen as the manifestation or creation of individual personal differences projected onto an organization. As we shall argue later, differences in organizational structures can also affect differences in individual personality structures.

The exercise also helps give an interesting response to the question of where the stakeholders of Chapter Three come from. They not only "come out" of the social system per se but they also come out of the minds of individuals. It should not be surprising to find that STs and NTs instinctively and implicitly seem to use the positional, demographic, and focal organizational approaches in identifying stakeholders when presented with the opportunity to do so (see Chapter Three). Hence, they focus on and give special recognition to the stakeholders associated with these methods. NFs and SFs, however, instinctively and implicitly seem to use the imperative, reputational, social-participation, and opinion-leadership methods. They use, in other words, the methods that are in accord with their views of social reality. They see (recognize) the stakeholders that fit their views, and their views fit or reflect the kinds of stakeholders they recognize as legitimate.

If this is so, then it is vitally important to understand the linkages between personality differences of individuals and the views of social systems (realities) that different individuals construct. This is also why it is so important to have methods like those described in Chapter Two that allow individuals to explore the differences that exist among them. As real-world problems (as opposed to exercises) have become so complex, it is important to appreciate that all four styles or attitudes have a fundamental role to play in defining and resolving important issues. No one style or attitude is capable of recognizing or dealing with all of the significant features of "reality."

We have reached a critical point in our discussion. We can begin to see not only that there is a crucial link between the structure of individual personality and the structure of social systems but what the nature of that link is in some detail. To make this fundamental link more explicit requires, however, that we take another step in explicating the structure of the human personality. This step will allow us, finally, to show how the stakeholders that constitute the human mind at one level link up with the stakeholders that constitute a social system. This is the purpose of the next chapter.

Before we leave this chapter, however, four lists are presented. Each list shows explicitly the general issues and stakeholders that each of the four Jungian personality types is inclined to be most interested in. The lists are the result of collecting over the years the kinds of concerns that the different personality types, that is, practicing managers, express.

External-People or NF Concerns

1. There is a strong customer demand for our current products.

2. Our customers are loyal and are not likely to switch to other products.

3. The bargaining power of our customers is relatively weak. They are price takers.

4. This is an easy business to get into; there are relatively few barriers to new entries.

5. The intensity of competition in this business is high, almost cut-throat.

6. Our major suppliers do not have much bargaining power; generally we set the terms of purchase.
7. Government regulation is generally favorably inclined to this business.
8. Current government legislature favors this business.
9. Most community and public interest groups are in support of our business.
10. Our business is conducted in a way that is consistent with prevailing social and cultural values.
11. Political action constitutes no threat to this business.
12. Our products, facilities, publications, and the ways we conduct business are aesthetically pleasing.
13. The media like us. We get good press.
14. Our business and our products are above reproach, morally and ethically.
15. Our business is in keeping with prevailing religious and other belief systems.
16. Our business is free from outside labor and political organizers such as Saul Alinsky who seek to organize our workers and change our methods.
17. Our business is free from outsiders such as Ralph Nader who seek to modify our products.
18. We have no need to fear outsiders period; we even welcome them.
19. Our business is basically free from foreign competition.
20. The average citizen has a great deal of respect for our industry.
21. The average citizen respects our products and our methods of doing business.
22. Our business is well-respected in the communities in which we do business.
23. All of the allied businesses upon which our business depends are supportive of us.

External-Technical or NT Concerns

1. There are no substitutes for our product.
2. It is unlikely that someone else will produce a new technological innovation that will render our current products obsolete.

3. It is unlikely that someone else will produce a new technological innovation that will materially affect our production process, volumes, quality, and costs.
4. Our product life cycle will not change.
5. Our business has adequate sources of raw material supplies for its operation.
6. Our cost of obtaining raw materials is competitive.
7. This business is able to secure all of the financial resources it needs at competitive rates.
8. There are many new markets available into which our business might reasonably expand.
9. There are many new products and services that our business might reasonably offer.
10. Our business is closely monitoring new technological developments that might affect our products and processes.
11. We have good access to new technological developments as they occur.
12. There are ample merger and acquisition opportunities available to our business.
13. The future looks bright for our business.
14. Economic conditions are favorable for our business.
15. Our business possesses great innovation abilities; R and D is likely to come up with new products and processes.
16. We lead the industry in product and service innovation.

Internal-People or SF Concerns

1. There is good communication among people and departments in our business.
2. Everyone here gets along well.
3. Our sales force is strong.
4. Our field support staff is superb.
5. The business is effective in attracting, hiring, and retaining qualified personnel.
6. The business is effective in developing, educating, and training personnel.
7. Our employees' attitudes, motivation, and dedication toward the business are strong assets.
8. Our employees are satisfied.

9. This is a safe place to work.
10. On the whole our employees are very healthy.
11. On the whole our managers are very healthy.
12. This business gives people great opportunities for personal growth.
13. The spouses and families of everyone who works here are happy and secure.
14. Our turnover is very low.
15. Our absenteeism is very low.
16. Our products and services are of the highest quality.

Internal-Technical or ST Concerns

1. The business is liquid, has enough cash reserves and flow to conduct business effectively.
2. The business is profitable.
3. We have an adequate market share.
4. We have an adequate inventory of (a) raw materials and (b) finished goods.
5. Our existing productive facilities are competitive on a cost and quality basis.
6. Our facilities are flexible enough to respond effectively to changes in our supply markets or product mix.
7. Our facilities are easily expandable to handle increased workload.
8. Our holdings of land, buildings, and equipment are quite valuable on the open market.
9. The productivity of our business is very high.
10. Our return on investment is substantial.
11. We enjoy a comparatively large market share in our markets.
12. Our business is effective in purchasing, designing, or acquiring the necessary equipment and facilities for producing our products and services.
13. Our business is very effective in acquiring the financial resources it needs.
14. Management is effective at (a) planning, (b) staffing, (c) controlling, (d) coordinating, (e) directing and leading, (f) making decisions, and (g) informing.

Note that for reasons of space I can only state the concerns in their most generic form. Many of the statements would obviously have to be refined to apply in a particular situation. Nevertheless, they show the direct bearing of the previous discussion on the management of complex social systems. Also note that, as they are written, they primarily apply to private institutions. With little modification, they could be rewritten to apply to public institutions as well. Note further that many of the items are idealized. As such, they are extremely contentious. For instance, in the first list it is not clear that items 16 and 17 should be answered in the affirmative. That is, it is far from clear that this should be the goal of every business. The items have been included to encourage explicit debate: do they, should they apply to a particular organization? If so, why? To what extent? Also note that many of the items apply to more than one of the lists. Although an item could fit equally well in more than one list, its sense or interpretation will be different from list to list.

CHAPTER FIVE

The Ego
as Stakeholder

The millions of personality multiples that make up the personality are shaped out of self and others as viewed through parents, brothers and sisters, relatives, animals, and inanimate objects [Sheikh and Jordan, 1981, p. 277].

To reach the next level of stakeholders, it is necessary to go beyond the typology of Chapter Four. We have to dig even deeper into the nature and the structure of the psyche. One of the ways to do this is to combine the insights of the previous chapter with another system. In this chapter we do two things: we explore the psychological system of Eric Berne and we explore the implications of what occurs when we combine the Jungian personality types with those of Berne. Both systems are really ego psychologies; that is, they reveal those aspects of the psyche that are closest to the surface. However, paradoxically, something strange occurs when we combine two systems that supposedly treat only the surface features of the psyche. Some of the deeper, that is, more unconscious, features begin to emerge or peek through the so-called ego levels of the mind.

All Types Are Not the Same

One of the most offensive things about any typology is that it "types" people, a consideration that Jung was painfully aware of and went to great lengths to avoid. Throughout his various descriptions of the types, he repeatedly cautions against putting people into "neat little boxes." This is not the purpose of his typology. Its fundamental purpose is to give people a framework and a series of concepts—a vocabulary—for recognizing and understanding their differences (Jung, 1968). The typology is not meant to impose a rigid classification of personality types nor does it imply permanent fixity throughout one's life. All sensing-thinking types are no more alike in all their features and characteristics than are all intuitive-feeling types, and so forth.

One way to see this is to combine Jung's types with those of Eric Berne, the father of transactional analysis. The thought occurred to me in pondering Berne's system that one reason sensing-thinking (ST) differs from person to person is that a person's conscious psychological function takes on a very different expression and operation depending on which of Berne's three characters it manifests itself through, the Parent, Adult, or Child.

To make Freud's concept of the ego more accessible to a wider audience, Berne replaced it with the concept of Parent, Adult, and Child. In effect, these three characters may be thought of as internal stakeholders, which, along with the Jungian types of the last chapter, make up the *first level* of the structure of the mind. It is important to realize that, although there are some overlaps, Berne's concepts of Parent, Adult, and Child do not correspond exactly to Freud's superego, ego, and id. There are superego, ego, and id aspects to every one of Berne's three characters. The relationship between Freud and Berne is thus more complex than is commonly supposed.

Before proceeding further, I should note that I have a number of reservations about Berne's system, which I shall discuss at the end of this chapter. Thus, I am anything but an unqualified advocate of the system. Nevertheless, I use the system because it is in accordance with my strong commitment to phenomenology. That is, it allows the general populace to see more directly the influence of deeper personality influences on their behavior and that of others.

The Parent embodies two distinct clusters of attributes. We can say also that the character of the Parent is bifurcated or contains two subcharacters: a nurturing or protective Parent and a critical or judging Parent. The protective Parent is basically nourishing and supportive. It provides the basic foundation for the development of the individual as a healthy ego. The critical Parent, however, serves no less a necessary role. If the Parent were wholly nourishing, then the individual would never become separate, that is, an autonomous individual. This judging character or part of the personality is easily observed whenever a person speaks of strict rights and wrongs.

It is important to appreciate that the "Parent" aspect of the personality initially resides wholly outside of the individual, that is, within one's original parents. Only later, as the individual develops, does the "Parent" aspect of the individual's personality develop. Initially, the personality or psyche of the individual is all "Child." Transactional analysis (TA) postulates further that there are various kinds of children within the Child. The first character, the original Child, is that of the "natural Child," which is closest to that of the nurturing Parent. It is warm, spontaneous, and all-giving as much as it is all-receiving and all-demanding. The "adapted Child," the first version of "the Parent in the Child," develops later. This is the socialized Child, the Child that has been molded by the parents to behave, get along, be nice, and so on. Another character, the "creative Child," also begins to develop at this time. This is the character that fantasizes about constantly obtaining the instinctual pleasures of the basic natural Child. When put to good use, this is the creative side of the human personality. When used negatively, it imposes a nearly autocratic demand to have everyone in the environment meet one's needs.

Finally, the Adult is the character whose often thankless task is to mediate the conflicting demands between the Parent and the Child sides of the personality. If the Child is all instinctual wish and fantasy (unbounded demand) and the Parent is all control (limits), then the Adult is the character that seeks to mediate between the two. The Adult forms plans and engages in action (reality testing) to secure pleasure or satisfy basic needs for the Child within the constraints of the Parent (morality, the law, society, and so on). Hence, the Adult, like all the characters, has at least two basically conflicting sides or aspects. On the one hand, it is a mediator between two strong characters, and hence it is subject to them. On the other hand, it has its own separate life to lead in meeting and testing reality.

The link between Jung and Berne is as follows. If a person were an ST in the conscious mode but were guided by underlying unconscious forces of the Parent mode, then the person's attitude, often expressed, would be that *only* the ST version of reality was valid. All other attitudes would be viewed as wrong. If, however, one's ST were under the influence of the Child, then depending upon which one of Berne's Child characters was operating, one would feel either inferior, small, and helpless or so wildly creative and uninhibited that others might have extreme difficulty in understanding one's thoughts. If, finally, one's ST were guided by the Adult subcharacter or aspect of the personality, then one's attitude would be entirely different. The Adult is the character whose ego is presumably developed enough to deal realistically with the world. Notice that we did not say "developed enough to deal realistically with reality," for each type's conscious function is, for all practical purposes, "reality" for that type. Hence, there is little breaking out of the circle except through the recognition that reality consists of the bringing together of the "realities" of the other types. But this is precisely the attitude of the Adult subcharacter which, in effect, says: "I have my way of viewing the world and to me it often seems so natural that there could be no other way; but others are just as convinced of their way; if it is not an either/or, if others do not represent a threat to me as they do to the Parent or Child, then the questions I must ask myself are: 'What can I learn from and give to others? How can we combine our different visions of the world to achieve a more powerful one?' "

In essence, the thought that occurred to me was that the Parent, Adult, and Child characters could be overlaid on the Jungian personality dimensions to achieve a richer framework to better understand human behavior. Lest the significance of this be lost or undermined, let me make my point somewhat differently. One of the great strengths of the Tinkertoy exercise and the stakeholder approach to social system analysis and design is that they allow people of different education, intellectual ability, temperament, and training to *see* one of the most difficult of all phenomena to witness—personality, that is, inner differences. Tinkertoy constructions and stakeholder parties are concrete entities. So are Berne's three characters. The author belives that we, as social scientists, have a deep responsibility to help others observe, *in their own terms and words,* the phenomena of which they are fundamentally a part and hence constitute.

Integrating Jung and Transactional Analysis (TA)

A careful reading of Jung in light of the TA system shows that the description of the Jungian personality types is heavily related to the TA character types. That is, Jung constantly mixes his descriptions of the personality types with aspects of the Parent, Adult, and Child. In part, this is because the Jungian personality types do not have an existence independent of or separate from the three characters of Parent, Adult, or Child. For instance, there is nothing in the nature of ST that makes it more or less amenable to any one of the three characters. Indced, ST can function in or be colored by any one of the three TA modes. Noting exactly which one of the three TA types is coloring a particular Jungian type helps to define more precisely the dynamics of personality.

This last point is exceedingly important, for it is often thought—mistakenly—that Thinking is the exclusive province or function of the Adult and Feeling that of the Child. This view is mistaken in that children are capable of primitive thought processes. By the same token, adults are capable of primitive feelings. An Einstein and a child can both be said to "think" although at very different levels of performance. Both functions are susceptible to different degrees of development and/or quality.

Figure 5 shows in greater detail one of the many possible patterns of interaction between the two systems. It shows a typical pattern of "normal" development and adaptation. A

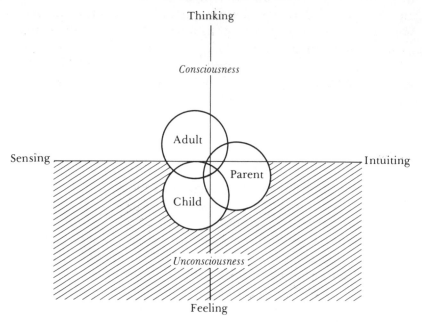

Figure 5. Combining the Jungian and TA Types:
A Normal State of Development.

personality structure in which the person's dominant decision style is that of ST is illustrated. That is, ST is the person's normal, Adult style of relating to reality. All those aspects of the person that are relatively undeveloped, that is, in a primitive and archaic state, are in the unconscious or, in Jungian terms, in the person's shadow.

In terms of Jungian theory this means that the person's Child and Parent characters are at least partly in the opposite personality quadrant, NF. The reason is that if by definition the Adult most clearly represents the most consciously developed and adapted psychological function, then the Parent and the Child represent the functions most closely tied to the unconscious. Not only are the Parent and the Child the first aspects of the psyche to emerge from a general state of unconsciousness, but they are the characters that remain most under the influence of the person's unconscious (the original Child) and the

unconscious of the original parents. As Jung and a strong body
of clinical evidence show, the unconscious speaks through the
"original, Childlike and Parentlike" characters in all of us.

The point is that if the Adult is generally to be found in
one's preferred or dominant style of orientation toward reality,
then the Parent or Child are to be found, if only partially, in the
psychological function most removed from or opposed to one's
dominant function. In short, *it is not possible for all three characters to exist or to operate to the same* conscious *degree in any
one of the Jungian quadrants.*

Combination of the two systems leads one to postulate
that personality is governed by three general factors:

1.   The "size" of the three TA characters or circles relative to
     one another
2.   Their "location" relative to one another in relation to the
     Jungian dimensions
3.   The "nature" of the intersections between the circles inter-
     preted psychologically

Thus, Figure 5 indicates a condition wherein the Adult is
the psychological character that is the most consciously developed. Parts of the Parent have also developed into consciousness. This means that the person is somewhat aware of the Parent side of his or her personality, for example, when he or she
uses it, why, and so on. Second, the Child is the character
which, in this particular case, is most embedded in the region of
the unconscious. Third, and perhaps most important, there is a
substantial *positive intersection* among the three characters. Indeed, without substantial positive intersection the Adult side of
the person could not have developed as much as it has. Unless
the person has achieved some minimal degree of harmony with
his or her Parent and Child, the Adult will not develop to its
fullest.

The meaning of the intersection is that although the person's primary orientation toward consciousness is ST, the person
is not completely at the mercy of the unconscious NF and SF
parts of the personality. Thus, for instance, if the natural Child

in particular represents the creative side of the personality, then the person portrayed in Figure 5 will be able to draw on his or her creative side through contact with these other characters. The unconscious sides of the personality, although still unconscious and therefore still relatively undeveloped, unassimilated, or primitive, will not be as foreign, removed, or strange and therefore as threatening if there were no points of contact whatsoever. In short, they will be better *integrated* into the entire structure of the personality.

This point is crucial because TA generally regards intersection between the characters as a condition of *infection* or *contamination*. That is, the normal personality is supposedly represented by three *non*intersecting circles. This is meant to indicate that each subcharacter is alive and well and functioning on its own almost as an autonomous self-contained individual. Now clearly more is at stake here than getting hung up on the particular mode of representing the normal personality, that is, whether by circles, squares, or boxes and the degree of *geometric* overlap between them. What seems to have been missed in the TA concept is that intersection can stand just as legitimately for two conditions, neither of which is necessarily exclusive. The first condition is that of *integration,* the second is that of *infection.*

There are three possible kinds of infection or contamination. The first case is where the messages or uncontrolled impulses of the Parent infect the Adult. An example is where the Parent believes that "all the members of a certain race or class make bad or unreliable employees." The Adult, however, may actually know and respect a "reliable member of the race" in question. The effect may be the barest minimum of compromise between the two. That is, the Adult may settle for the statement, "The person I know is the rare exception to the general rule." This kind of compromise, if it can be called that, is known as *prejudice.*

But notice that it could have worked the other way around. The Adult could have exercised a greater hold or sense of power on the Parent and caused the Parent to soften its extreme all-or-nothing stand even further. That is, the Adult could have educated the Parent by forcing reality testing, the thing that the Adult supposedly does all too well. This is the sense in which intersection can stand for integration and not just contamination. The thing we are dealing with, the human psyche, is so complex that it is terribly easy to overlook or to mistake its workings, even by the most sensitive students of the subject. As Jung himself said repeatedly throughout his many writings, the psyche is the means (instrument) by which we learn of the psyche. As a result, there is no such thing in any aspect of human affairs as purely disinterested, objective knowledge (and this includes knowledge in the physical sciences as well) (Mitroff, 1974). All knowledge is infected and contaminated to an inevitable degree by the unconscious workings (projections) of our minds (psyches) onto the structure of other minds (psyches).

A second kind of contamination is that of the Child and the Adult. A classic example is that of a business that is so infatuated (Child) with its product, call it the Edsel, that it ignores reality (Adult). It denies its own market research which indicates unequivocally that there is no real market for a car with such an unappealing, if not comic, name. The best name for this kind of contamination is *delusion*. That is, the Adult (reality) is deluded by the forceful feelings (fantasies) of the Child.

A third type is the Parent/Child contamination. An example of this is when the repressive ideology (Parent) of a business hinders it from going into new business with obvious fun, creative aspects (Child), for example, the entertainment or luxury car business. The original Ford as produced by Henry is an example of this. You could have any color you wanted as long as it was black. The best compromise that may be struck here is to go into the creative business but suffer feelings of guilt. This case is called *confusion* in the TA literature.

A further example may help. Consider the case of an executive who comes up with a long list of artificial-sounding, that is, an overrationalized, set of reasons for buying a new gadget (say, a computer) which the business really does not need (as judged from an Adult perspective). In this case, the true motive is that of the Child who wants the prestige of owning or playing with an expensive toy, that is, of having fun. If the executive were in better touch with his or her Child, then the less the Child would have to speak through the Adult and, as a result, the character actually speaking or running the show could be recognized. The situation could be dealt with in a more realistic manner, and hence, actually more rationally.

As is well known from a large body of clinical evidence, the more that a critical aspect of the personality is suppressed or repressed, the greater is the chance that that which is denied or buried in the psyche will exert an even greater force in proportion upon consciousness. Strangely, the point is that *the farther down into one's shadow or unconsciousness the Child and the Parent are pushed or buried, the greater the influence they exert over the supposedly conscious, Adult function.* Indeed, we can say that in the particular case that the Child and/or Parent are buried, the greater chance there is of their enveloping the Adult. That is, even though the Adult (that is, the ego) is the voice through which consciousness generally speaks, the message or the dialogue may actually be written and dictated by the unconsciousness (see Figure 6). That is, the Adult may be so overwhelmed by the Parent and Child that it may have no voice independent of these two characters (Figure 6). Alternatively, the Adult (or any of the other two states) may be so underdeveloped, that it may have little if any existence or bearing on one's outer behavior.

The concept of underdevelopment leads to a discussion of the various mechanisms by which one mind or psyche affects another. From psychoanalytic theory (see Corsini, 1979, 1981), it is well known that there are a number of such mechanisms, only a few of which we can discuss here. They include, among many, compensation, contamination, identification, introjection, projection, and symbiosis. There are a number of different senses and meanings to the term *compensation.* In terms of the preceding discussion, one form of compensation is the process by which the psyche attempts to counter its own tendency toward narrowness or one-sidedness. For example, if one is an extreme thinking type who tends to intellectualize everything, then he or she may be more susceptible to those aspects of the psyche (for example, Parent or Child) that express neglected or

Figure 6. Envelopment by the Child and Parent.

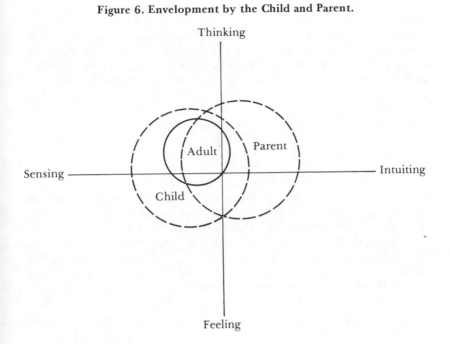

underdeveloped feeling or emotional aspects of the person's personality (Jung, 1973).

We have already touched on contamination and the difficulty of often distinguishing it from its close psychological relative, integration. Identification and introjection, while closely related to one another and to contamination, can be distinguished from one another nonetheless. As part of the process of growing up, as a result of the deep and prolonged emotional and physical dependency of the child on the parents (Brown, 1959), and as a fundamental by-product of becoming socialized and thereby "human," the child at first *merges* and *identifies* so strongly with the parents or their substitutes that he or she *introjects* or takes into his or her own personality, parts of the parents' personalities. To be honest, we still do not fully comprehend or understand the process or mechanism of introjection. Wilber (1981b) has given one of the best treatments of this process of which I know:

The male child wants to possess the mother so as to complete the body unity; that is, he wants to see himself with his mother, and thus he wants to "oust" the father. . . . The child wants to pry the parents apart and thus step in himself with the mother and close the body circle. This is of course impossible, and so, through a rather complicated course whose details need not concern us, the child takes the next-best thing and *identifies* with the father, since the father *already* possesses the mother. The boy more or less surrenders the desire to *possess* the mother and seeks instead to be *like* the father ("identifications replace object-choices").

But identification is a *mental* accomplishment. The child can identify with the father only by using concepts, roles, and so on. And this means a fundamental transformation has occurred from body union to mental union. The child does not take the actual father into his body, he takes the father image into his ego. (This is also part of the formation of the superego, the internalized parent.) This overall identification helps the child form a higher-order self, a properly mental self, and a strong ego capable of more than body-bound desires [p. 223].

All we know through countless case studies of childhood and adulthood is that introjection occurs (Wickes, 1966). The child takes in characters from the parents' own psyche or character structure and then forms his or her own unique character structure. Another way to put this is to say that one's own actual parents contribute to the formation of the Parent character within one's own character structure (Klein, 1980).

Projection is the process whereby a person projects inner psyche states onto another person, object, or even animal. For example, if your decision style or personality is so different from mine, then I may be likely to project *unacknowledged, and undesired,* aspects of myself onto you. *If you and I are in a competitive relationship and I have some long-standing issues connected with competitiveness that express themselves in the form of fear or anxiety, then I may be likely to project my fears onto you as characteristic properties of you, not me.* This is why, again for many reasons, it is so difficult to obtain a true picture of the stakeholders in one's environment. The picture one has is always colored, to some extent, by the mechanism of projection. The knowledge of "the extent" (that is, degree) can be had only by involving someone skilled in reading and decoding psychological messages. The argument here is that as the complexity of the environment has grown enormously, the opportunity for unconscious projections to operate has also grown enormously. Furthermore, the analysis of the operation of such mechanisms is no longer a luxury but a vital necessity if one is to manage, that is, effectively deal with, the complex array of forces that impinges on the modern large-scale organization.

Finally, we discuss one last mechanism, symbiosis. If the introjection between persons is so enveloping and strong, then we may speak of a symbiotic relationship. This occurs when an ego-state of one person substitutes or functions for an ego-state of another. An example is when the Parent (or Adult) of one person functions as the Parent (or Adult) for another person whose own Parent is either nonexistent or underdeveloped (see Figure 7). We quote: "In a *symbiotic* relationship, a mother

Figure 7. An Example of Symbiosis.

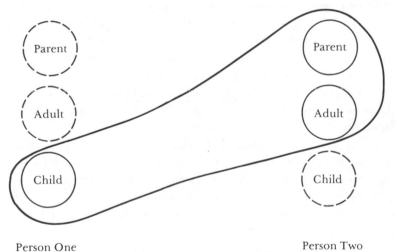

Person One   Person Two

[Person Two in Figure 7] and her child [Person One] become intimately linked in a mutually dependent way, and they behave as a *single* individual, usually the mother functions as the operating Parent and Adult, and her offspring maintains only the Child ego-state. In other words, two persons are operating as one complete individual in a symbiotic relationship. Symbiosis is normal during infancy; later it is seen as pathological" (Dusay and Dusay, 1979, p. 398).

Recapitulation and Conclusion

Because of the complexity and the number of the ideas introduced in the last two chapters, it is necessary to present a review of the central thrust of the overall argument. Chapter Four presented a discussion of the personality differences that can be observed between people. These differences constitute what is known as a person's cognitive decision style. As such, these are the aspects of a person's personality that exist near the surface of the psyche. More precisely, a person's dominant psychological style or type is conscious. Those aspects that are less dominant lie further beneath the surface, that is, in the person's shadow or unconscious.

Next it was shown how the Jungian personality system that was originally developed as a powerful tool for explicating the structure of the individual personality can be extended as a powerful tool for analyzing organizational structure. In effect, it was shown that different types of organizations can be understood as arising from the projections of different personality structures.

It was shown that different psychological types have a tendency to concentrate on different types of social system stakeholders. Thus, stakeholders as well as organizations can in part be viewed as the projections of different psychological types. This does not mean that stakeholders at the social system level are nothing but the projections of different psychological types. It merely means that individual psychology plays an important, if not indispensable, *part* in the perception, existence, and maintenance of organizations. As I shall argue later, it also works the other way around. The structure of external organizations and institutions can play an important part in the creation and maintenance of individual personality structure.

Through the use of a system known as Transactional Analysis (TA), it was shown in this chapter that the layers of the psyche just below a person's cognitive decision style or surface personality structure can be construed as a miniature social system. Namely, personality is not merely cognitive style alone but the *interaction between* decision style *and* three subcharacters or internal stakeholders, Parent, Adult, and Child. In turn, each of the three subcharacters can interact *between them* in a number of ways. We begin to see the "why," if not the "how," of the complexity of human behavior.

Our examination has also revealed an alternate, if not deeper, set of ways in which one stakeholder can influence another. These ways include such psychological mechanisms as compensation, contamination, identification, introjection, projection, and symbiosis. These mechanisms stand in sharp contrast to those discussed in Chapter Three. The mechanisms in Chapter Three were, for the most part, "rational." As such, they were *supposedly* under the rational control of a decision maker, that is, supposedly one could choose rationally whether to employ one mechanism or not. For instance, some people think they can choose whether or not to fall in love so as to marry for money, power, prestige, and so forth.

The mechanisms discussed in this chapter, however, are not rational in the sense that they can not be consciously chosen. This does not necessarily make them irrational but nonrational; that is, they do not obey the same kinds of laws or principles as do the mechanisms for influencing or changing stakeholders discussed in Chapter Three. It will be recalled that the kinds of laws that operate at the level discussed in Chapter Three were that of rational, if-then principles. For example, "*if* the environment is such and such, *then* an organization ought to raise its prices to compete effectively against other stakeholders, and so on."

We have taken the first step in the creation of a psychosocial theory of management. I have argued, in effect, that individuals project an aspect of their psychic structure (the interaction between their decision style plus TA character structure) *onto* the external stakeholders in their environment. Little wonder that it is so difficult to discuss objectively the true nature of one's organization and its environment. Also little wonder that individuals often differ so markedly in their characterization of the very same organization.

Finally, I have also argued by implication that organizations and institutions have a character structure of their own. If it is certainly the case that organizations differ noticeably in their *style,* for example, bureaucratic, matrix, and so on, then it is also the case that they differ markedly in the *character* that they project to the outside world. Certainly it can be said that some organizations have a definite Parent character. One literally has to get permission to do just about anything (for example, go to the restroom); strict rules exist with regard to everything.

A fascinating series of questions can be stated. One of the most critical phenomena that cuts across both the fields of organizational behavior and business policy is that of mergers and acquisitions. What does it mean from a behavioral standpoint, especially from the perspective with which we have been viewing it, for one organization to *merge* with another? When two or more stakeholders at the organizational and/or individual level merge or divest themselves which aspects of the various "selves" are merging/divesting? When two or more stakeholders affect an organizational/individual marriage/divorce, which aspects of the selves get married or get divorced? We know so little about these questions for any number of reasons. Since the questions themselves cut across traditional academic specialties (organizational psychology, sociology, psychiatry, business policy), we have only the barest hint of an answer in terms of the kinds of research that has been done to date (see Chapter Seven). Up to this point, psychologists and sociologists have examined only a few interactions between ego-states and institutions, but none across them. There certainly has not been anything approaching the study of interactions across the levels of human systems I am calling for. The questions themselves have hardly been raised. My purpose here cannot be, therefore, to answer them but to set a posture, a tone, which I hope raises them to importance—to consciousness, that is, an agenda for future inquiry. It should be noted in this regard that Wilber (1981b) is one of the

very few who have even recognized the problem: "Psychoanalytic theory fails to grasp that each level of the human com-
pound individual possesses a boundary or interface, and that
introjection and projection can and do occur across the boundaries of *any* level. . . . This [has occurred] because psychoanalysis takes the skin boundary of the organism as *the* fundamental
boundary, whereas it is the most visible. There are emotional
boundaries, membership boundaries, egoic boundaries, psychic
boundaries, and so on, and *each* supports traffic in internaliza-
tion (introjection) and alienation (projection)" (pp. 265–266).

Finally, I would like to stress once again that I am anything but an unqualified advocate of the TA system. I have a
great many reservations about it. In particular, like many other
people, I am often put off by its language. At times it reduces
to triteness the many profound insights of Freud. Furthermore,
unlike Freud, it does not go deep enough. Like so many of the
ego therapies, it even contends that one need not go further beneath the surface than it does. It almost dispenses with the very
concept of the unconscious.

My position is not that certain terms like the unconscious
are so holy that they cannot and need not be fundamentally re-
examined to see if they are still necessary. Instead, my point is
that TA and the other ego therapies do not go deep enough beneath the surface. They do not exhaust the full range of the
subcharacters or subpersonalities that constitute the deeper
structure of the human psyche. For this reason, they have not
shown that the concept of the unconscious is outworn or dis-
pensable. The concept of the unconscious is absolutely indispensable in understanding the complexity of the workings of
human institutions and, of course, the mind.

I have adopted TA in this chapter not because of any
deep or profound attachment to it but because, in spite of its
limitations, it is still the most concrete way I know of to give
the reader the most painless way into the probings of the deep
structure of human systems. If its language is frankly corny at
times, it is at least understandable and its points are easily
grasped. If the range of characters it treats is limited, this in itself is information about this brand of human systems analysis.

The limited range of stakeholders that is dealt with is generally indicative of the ego therapies.* Thus nothing is really gained by going to another therapy. One merely exchanges one limited set of characters for another. What is needed is a theory of the broadest set of stakeholder characters that compose the deepest layers and structure of the human mind. This is the task to which I turn in Chapter Six. In Chapter Seven I give some concrete examples to show how stakeholders are alive and functioning in all spheres of human activity.

---

*We quote: "Federn held that the *normal* ego was divided, dissociated into segments that assumed responsibility for different areas of behavior and experience, much as the individuals in a society specialize their contributions through different occupations. These subpatterns of personality he called *ego-states*. The normal ego, therefore, is similar to a nation with different geographical areas and jurisdictions such as states, counties, and so forth. The well-adjusted individual has a strong federal government, but different ego-states enable him or her to activate certain behaviors when at a party and others when at work. . . . An ego-state may be defined as a body of behaviors and experiences bound together by some common principle or function and separated from other such entities by a more or less permeable boundary. It has a semiautonomous existence within the entire personality. That state in which the largest amount of ego cathexis is invested at any time is said to be 'executive' " (Watkins and Watkins, 1981, p. 255).

 CHAPTER SIX

Archetypes:
Symbolic Images
Deep in the Mind

Early man—like the child—perceives the world "mythological-ly." That is, he experiences the world predominantly by form-ing archetypal images that he projects upon it. The child, for example, first experiences in his mother the archetype of the Great Mother, that is, the reality of an all-powerful . . . woman, on whom he is dependent in all things, and not the objective reality of his personal mother, this particular historical woman which his mother becomes for him later when his ego and con-sciousness are more developed. . . . Human life in the beginning is determined to a far higher degree by the unconscious than by consciousness; it is directed more by archetypal images than by concepts, by instincts than by the voluntary decisions of the ego; and man is more a part of his group than an individual [Neumann, 1955, pp. 15-16].

An Introduction to Archetypes

In the previous chapter we saw that the structure of a person's personality can be viewed as a miniature, internal social system. That is, the structure of a person's personality can be understood in terms of the characteristic properties and interac-tions between a small set of internal stakeholders. These special internal stakeholders constitute the "partial" structure of the psyche. I have deliberately emphasized the word *partial,* for as I argued at the end of Chapter Five, the cast of internal stakeholders that the various types of ego psychologies identify does not exhaust the full range of internal stakeholders that constitute the psyche. While the ego psychologies go deeper beneath the surface of everyday life than do the social systems analyses of stakeholders, they do not penetrate as deeply and broadly as is possible through other methods. The deepest layers of the psyche are composed of stakeholders that are more wondrous, fascinating, and even terrifying than either social system analyses or ego psychology have identified.

Long before the methods of social problem solving described in the previous chapters reached their current form of application and development, I embarked on a study of Jung's archetypal psychology. Out of this study emerged a deeper set of internal stakeholders that constitute the psyche.

Archetypes lie deeper within the formation and operation of the psyche than the kinds of internal stakeholders discussed in Chapters Four and Five. In addition to the Parent (or superego) aspect of one's psyche and one's own actual parents, there exists an archetypal, a general symbolic, concept of the parents. This aspect of the psyche is almost totally unknown to most people. As a result, its profound influence on human affairs is almost completely unseen or unacknowledged (Jung, 1973).

The archetypal concept of the parents is discussed and revealed in virtually all the great myths, legends, fairy tales, and religions of the world (Frye, 1973). As a result, however, it is the most symbolic and the most difficult to recognize, to fathom, and to understand. In brief, *an archetype is the most symbolic, universal psychological image of a character type known.* Jung says that "[the archetypes] exist preconsciously and presumably they form the structural dominants of the psyche in general. They may be compared to the invisible presence of the crystal lattice in a saturated solution" (cited in Neumann, 1963, p. 6). And Neumann says, "Not only does [an archetype] act as a magnetic field, directing unconscious behavior of the personality through the pattern of behavior set up by the instincts; it also operates as a pattern of vision in the consciousness, ordering the psychic material into symbolic images" (Neumann, 1963, p. 6). In other words, archetypes are the most basic, universal, human symbols through which humans experience the world (and themselves) and order the world of phenomena so that they are able to have experience.

Although archetypes can be observed in dreams in the form of mythological characters, they are most readily seen through an analysis of comparative world mythology, legends, fairy tales, religion, and so forth (Bettelheim, 1977; Campbell, 1979; Frye, 1973; Girard, 1977; Hillman, 1975b; Jacobi, 1959; Jung, 1973; Neumann, 1955, 1970; Nichols, 1980; Ogilvy, 1977; Propp, 1968; Slater, 1966). The more that one examines the great diversity of world cultures, the more one finds that at a symbolic level there is an astounding amount of agreement between various archetypal images (Neumann, 1955, 1970). People may disagree and fight one another by day but at night they show the most profound similarity in their dreams and myths. The agreement is too profound to be produced by chance alone. It is therefore attributed to a similarity of the psyche at the deepest layers of the unconscious. These similar appearing symbolic images are termed archetypes.

Why does the mind produce these images? What is their purpose, their function? While vitally important, these questions border on the meaningless. One is tempted to say, "Because that's the way the mind 'is,' " and let it go at that. However one responds, there will be a strong element of circularity. That is, the mind produces archetypes because that is its constitution.

From another perspective, however, the questions are not meaningless. At the most elemental level, archetypes exist to help a person develop an emotionally satisfying picture of the world. The world is so terrifying to the primitive and child that both need some way of coping with it, of organizing it (Jaynes, 1976). They cannot use the techniques available to the adult. They cannot psychologically distance themselves enough to give a disinterested, rational, or scientific picture of the world. Since the child and the primitive project their inner fears out onto the world, little wonder that some of the most universal and potent

archetypal images are of the strangest looking demons—half hu-
man-half animal creatures. Neumann writes: "In the early phase
of consciousness, the [strength] of the archetype ... exceeds
man's power of representation, so much so at first no form can
be given to it. And when later the primordial archetype takes
form in the imagination of man, its representations are often
monstrous and inhuman. This is the phase of the chimerical
creatures composed of different animals or of animal and man—
the griffins, sphinxes, harpies, for example—and also of such
monstrosities as phallic and bearded mothers. It is only when
consciousness learns to look at phenomena from a certain distance, to react more subtly, to differentiate and to distinguish,
that the mixture of symbols prevailing in the primordial archetype separates into the groups of symbols characteristic of a
single archetype or of a group of related archetypes; in short
that they become recognizable" (1955, pp. 12-13). Such beings
represent an individual's terrifying internal nature concretized
and projected out onto external reality in an attempt to cope
with his or her inner and outer fears.

Every aspect of a person's existence is capable of being
turned into an archetypal symbol, image, or character (McCully,
1971). Thus, there exists an archetypal mythological character
for every part of a person's psyche and social structure. As Ogilvy (1977) observes: "We moderns would do well to reflect on
the transformation of the [ancient] Trinity of Zeus, Apollo,
and Dionysus into their more recent mythological counterparts,
the superego, ego, and id" (p. 141). The key word in the preceding passage is *counterpart*. There exists a counterpart or corresponding archetype for every condition, experience, and aspect
of an individual. As McCully (1971) puts it:

We posit that the structure of *the psyche itself may be
something* like [the Rorschach] *inkblot structure*. Both the substance in Rorschach's inkblots and the substance of the psyche
itself provide the conditions which allow images to form around
stimuli that are potent enough to precipitate them. Inkblots are
as potent as their stimulus power. . . . We [call] that power
archetypal. . . .
An archetype, or image that represents it, . . . contains

the essence of a particular human experience that has been re-
peated enough to make a permanent but not necessarily unalter-
able print on neural structure. . . . It does not appear that archetypal patterns are necessarily fixed. Inherent capacities for
flexibility may be a chief difference between neural structure in
man and other animals. Nevertheless, some of our experiences
are so fundamental in existence that one cannot expect the human condition without them. . . .

Archetypes include such prototypal [basic human] experiences as food gathering, elimination, fertility, father, mother,
authority, self, femininity, goddess, eternity, childhood, circle,*
square, devil (evil), god (good), maleness, and sleep. If we look
at the core or essence of a symbol, according to laws pertaining
to subjective processes, we will find evidence for archetypal influences.

Since all men have created some form of religion no matter where they sprang up, religion should provide us with resi-
dues of concrete deposits of archetypal action. Christ and The
Buddha symbolize some essence of archetypal deposit for us,
since they are the religious representative of our era [p. 51].

There are archetypes corresponding to every kind of authority figure, to conditions of chance or uncertainty, war,
death, occupation, and so on. Numbers, too, can signify archetypes. Everything surrounding a person that can be used to give
order to his or her world is potentially capable of being experienced as an archetypal symbol. Consider the significance of the
number four. Nichols (1980) put together the following list of
some of the "fours" that order our thoughts:

> The four directions of the compass
> The four corners of the earth
> The four winds of heaven
> The four rivers of Eden
> The four qualities of the ancients (warm, dry, moist, cold)
> The four humours (sanguine, phlegmatic, choleric, melan-
>   cholic)
> The four apostles (Matthew, Mark, Luke, John)
> The four prophets (Isaiah, Jeremiah, Ezekiel, Hosea)

*The circle usually stands for completeness, wholeness—the contain-
ment of opposites. It is also one of the four basic geometric figures.

The four angels (Michael, Raphael, Gabriel, Phannel)

The four beasts of the Apocalypse

The four elements (earth, air, fire, water)

The four alchemical ingredients (salt, sulphur, mercury, azoth)

The four seasons

The four basic geometric figures (circle, line, square, triangle)

The four phases of the moon

The four Hebrew letters of the Lord's sacred name (Yod, He, Vau, He)

The four basic operations of arithmetic (addition, subtraction, multiplication, division)

The four cardinal virtues (justice, prudence, temperance, fortitude)

The list of "fours" that have helped man throughout the ages to direct his spiritual and physical life is endless. Four is also a number connected with the creation of man. The Syrian "Book of the Cave of Treasures" tells the story this way: "And they saw God take a grain of dust from the whole earth, and a drop of water from the whole sea, and a breath of wind from the upper air, and a little warmth from the nature of fire. And the angels saw how these four weak elements, the dry, the moist, the cold, and the warm, were laid in the hollow of his hand. And then God made Adam."

In summary, then, the number four symbolizes man's orientation to reality as a human being. One pictorial representation of the number four is a square, symbolic of the order superimposed by Logos on random nature [pp. 107-108].

Each archetype is an idealized image, more pure and extreme, and larger than life, to help us cope with and understand the complexities of life. Bettelheim puts it well in explaining the hold that fairy tales have on the mind of a child:

Contrary to what takes place in many modern children's stories, in fairy tales evil is as omnipresent as virtue. *In practically every fairy tale good and evil are given body in the form of some figures* and their actions, as good and evil, are omnipresent in life and the properties for both are present in every man [emphasis added]. It is this duality which poses the moral problem, and requires the struggle to solve it. . . .

The figures in fairy tales are not ambivalent—not good

and bad at the same time, as we all are in reality. But since po-
larization dominates the child's mind, it also dominates fairy
tales. A person is either good or bad, nothing in between. . . .
One parent is all good, the other evil. . . . Presenting the polari-
ties of character permits the child to comprehend easily the
differences between the two, which he could not do as readily
were the figures drawn more true to life, with all the complexities that characterize real people. Ambiguities must wait until
a relatively firm personality has been established on the basis of
positive identifications. Then the child has a basis for understanding that there are great differences between people, and
that therefore one has to make choices about who one wants to
be. This basic decision, on which all later personality developments will build, is facilitated by the polarizations of the fairy
tale [1977, pp. 8–9].

It would be a very grave mistake to think that such raw
images and projections are absent from the thought of adults. It
is undoubtedly true that the historical context of the vast majority of archetypes is by now so far removed from our direct
experience and daily lives that ancient traditional forms have
little if any contemporary meaning for us (Nichols, 1980). At
best, they appear bizarre, as if from another planet. At worst,
they seem to hopelessly degenerate into mysticism. And yet,
this is precisely the attitude we must avoid.

We need not regard archetypes as literally "real" (that is,
actual existing stakcholders) to take advantage of their usefulness, although in the next chapter we will examine some modern examples that are not only "real" but "actually existing."
The proper stance toward them is to see them as naturally occurring social projective tests so that we may better understand
ourselves (recall the earlier quote from McCully, 1971). In *The
Gamesman,* Maccoby (1976) reminds us that such images naturally and automatically crop up in organizational life; as such,
they afford us a unique, if not novel, way of understanding organizations and their impact on individuals and vice versa:

One of Goodwin's [a "company man"] Rorschach responses expressed the contradiction and the lack of grounding
for his goals. He saw fish, which he associated with the Chris-
tian faith, tied to a couple of court jesters teetering on the top

of two docking spaceships. This symbolized his approach to corporate policy, an unstable combination of Christianity [see the earlier quote from McCully] and the politics of the impotent courtier resting on technology in outer space. (The court fool tells the truth, but he is powerless.) He also expressed the contraction between the principles of religion and power in the two historical figures he most admired: "Alexander the Great, he affected the future and was a great leader, but understood people and how to bring them together. And Jesus [see McCully, 1971, p. 51] he changed man without force, showed the power of working with people" (p. 96).

The Properties of Archetypes

Of all the aspects of archetypes, none are more puzzling or strange than their detailed properties. The properties are best approached through the following series of questions: Is the number of archetypes limited or not? That is, can they be organized in terms of a basic set, a table, or a closed typology? How do they operate? What is the relationship between them? Are they separate entities or are some contained in others? A consideration of these questions will allow us to answer the most important question of all: What is the interrelationship among the stakeholders in terms of which the different levels of human reality are experienced and organized?

As the work of Maccoby (1976) shows, the internal organization of the psyche is not solely confined to one's inner life. Archetypes mirror experiences external to the individual as much as they filter and organize the internal experiences. There is an overlap between the inner structure of one's internal psyche and the outer structure of external organizations that influence the mind. The point is that there is a constant and strong interplay between the structure of the internal personality of an individual and the structure of the external environment. I quote from Maccoby:

The Rorschach responses of executives suggested that one of their most repressed feelings is humiliation at having to perform for others—from parents and teachers in childhood to the admired superiors at work—to be vulnerable and judged by them no matter how much the corporate policy emphasizes "respect for the individual." For example, on [Rorschach] Card II, a corporate [VP] first saw two performing elements, symbolizing strong and proud animals that had been trained and humbled. His next response was running tears of blood, symbolizing sadness, impotence, powerlessness, followed by rocket exhaust and flames, symbolizing phallic resistance, anger, hardening. He agreed with me that they represented the experience of castration and that it had led to compensatory toughness. Unlike the farmer or craftsman, the manager always remains in some way the school boy who is being judged on his performance [Maccoby, 1976, p. 117].

Two of the most systematic and extensive treatments of archetypal images can be found in the works of Nichols (1980), and Neumann (1955, 1970). Nichols analyzes in painstaking detail the twenty-two major symbols that compose the deck of Tarot cards. She shows that they can be organized in a format that comes tantalizingly close to a "periodic table of the human elements." The "elements" parallel and elaborate on the archetypes mentioned by McCully in the passage cited earlier. The full set of Tarot archetypes is as follows (followed by very brief descriptions: (1) the Fool (who bursts forth unexpectedly into our lives and thus fools us as well as others); (2) the Magician (symbolizing the unfathomable mystery and never-ending wonder of "it all"); (3) the High Priestess (symbolizing the Virgin); (4) the Empress (the Mother Archetype); (5) the Emperor (the Father Archetype); (6) the Pope (the Archetypal Wise Old Man or authority figure); (7) the Lover (the youthful ego separated from the mother and father archetypes but not yet fully developed and hence able to stand completely alone); (8) the Chariot (a vehicle to carry the hero, the young ego, on his journey to self-development); (9) Justice (the delicate and difficult feat of balancing between opposing principles of equal merit to secure rightness); (10) the Hermit (the deep voice within us all that needs to withdraw in order to find our individuality and renewal); (11) the Wheel of Fortune (the never-ending cycle of nature); (12) Force or Strength (the ambivalence of power, life-giving as well as destructive); (13) the Hanged Man (suspension, lack of progress); (14) Death (sudden change, finality, loss, end, surprise); (15) Temperance (a helpful, energy renewing figure); (16) the Devil (the grotesque and sinister side of our unconscious that remains in its original, undeveloped savage state); (17) the Tower of Destruction (rising illumination); (18) the Star (brightness); (19) the Moon (caution, danger); (20) the Sun (warmth, triumph, success); (21) Judgment (rebirth, decision, opportunity); (22) the World (completion, individuation, development, fulfillment, synthesis).

One of the most extensive in-depth analyses of a single archetype, the Feminine, is that by Neumann (1963). Neumann shows that there are many symbols or symbolic expressions that stand for the Feminine, not just one. Even more important, there is not a single Feminine archetype, but many, each one standing for the various aspects of the Feminine. Thus there are archetypes that stand for the creative and nourishing (that is, nurturing) aspects of the Female. Similarly, there are archetypes that stand for the destructive and devouring aspects of the Female, for example, the aspects of the Mother that will devour the child if it does not learn to break away and become independent at some point in its development. If the child does not separate and become a separate functioning person, it will fall back into a symbiotic state of union with the Mother. It will dissolve and lose its independent existence. Little wonder the mileposts of becoming an independent human are so fraught with terrible images: the process is an often frightening struggle.

One of the most incredible accomplishments of Neumann (1963) is his discovery that there is a kind of "typology" around which at least the Feminine archetype can be organized. However, it is a radically different kind of typology of stakeholders than those presented in the previous chapters. Unlike the typologies that typically underlie the so-called rational social system stakeholders, *the number of archetypes is neither fixed, constant, nor static.* Furthermore, they are neither exclusive nor exhaustive. Archetypal images are themselves neither fixed, constant, nor static. New archetypes are continually being made and altered as humanity shapes and remakes itself. We can attempt to take a static snapshot of some of the basic experiences around which archetypes form, but we cannot fix the basic number or the form of archetypes. Indeed, one of the archetypes that always seems to form just when we think we have captured the "complete set of archetypes" is an archetype having to do with precariousness, randomness, danger, and/or incompleteness. This archetype seems to function to alert us that the psyche may never fully succeed in fathoming itself *in fixed, static form.* Similarly, another closely accompanying archetype that also always seems to form is that of the Trickster (Jung, 1973). The Trickster tries to deceive us in any way possible, for example, by being that part of our psyche that lulls us into believing that we know all about ourselves (that we know the full set of archetypes) and then relishes suddenly bringing us up short to expose our arrogance and our ignorance.

While we can gain considerable insight into the broad outlines of the full range of archetypes, complete and definitive knowledge of the full set seems unopen to mortals. Indeed, such knowledge is only open to the Gods, one of humanity's earliest and most enduring of archetypes (Jaynes, 1976). *Complete knowledge, like perfection itself, is an attribute of an archetype. It is not a property of humanity.*

While all this is true, Chapter Nine argues that there may be an order to archetypes. However, this "order" is so bound up with philosophical speculations that it is best discussed there. That is, the kind of order that archetypes obey is itself an archetype, an archetypal conception of knowledge.

The further one delves into the nature of archetypes, the stranger their properties become. As we saw in Chapter Three, stakeholders at the level of the social system do not typically contain contradictory properties. At the very least, they attempt to avoid contradictions. This property is generally *not* characteristic of archetypes. Although there is a tendency for archetypal images to split into good versus bad, strong versus weak, nurturing versus devouring aspects, as the earlier quote from Bettelheim shows, the split is never complete. Thus, archetypes follow a logic that is very different from that which typifies the elements of "rational" social systems analysis. Ogilvy has perceived this best of all. He writes:

[The Presocratic Greek philosopher] Anaxagoras saw the next step more clearly than most [social analysts] do today. Eleatic philosophy *illicitly* [emphasis added] extends the logic of visual-tactile [senses] to the logic of concepts . . . the fact that two physical bodies cannot be in the same *place* at the same time is carried over into a much broader principle of non-contradiction [for all things] . . . a physical object cannot be both round and square in the same dimension at the same time, but it is perfectly possible [for a person, and certainly, an archetype] to be both generous and stingy, both loving and hating, both downcast and elated in quite the same respects at the same time, viz., the experience of dramatic tragedy. Just because perceptual space knows no ambivalence it does not follow that all ambivalence is a sign of contradictions to be eradicated in the lucidity of clear vision [1977, pp. 205-206].

In short, when we are dealing with a phenomenon as complex as a human being, we are not dealing with an entity that is free from contradiction. Contradiction *is* one of the essential characteristic properties of people, groups, organizations, and institutions. All of the archetypes contain contradictory properties or aspects. The Mother is weak *and* strong, loving *and* devouring. An organization can be both big *and* small, weak *and* strong, beautiful *and* ugly, and so forth, at the same time (Churchman, 1971; Mitroff and Kilmann, 1978; Mitroff and Mason, 1981a).

Finally we come to what may be the strangest property of all. *In principle, each archetype is contained within all the other archetypes. If the psyche structure of a human being is made up of archetypes,* then *the psyche of each archetype is itself made up of all the other archetypes.* This is why if an archetype has a dominant set of somewhat seemingly consistent properties, it also has a set of contradictory properties that "intrude" from the other parts of *its* psyche makeup (see Figure 8).

The principle is Leibnitzian and goes back to the early Greek philosophers: *Each slice of nature is contained within every other slice of nature.* While such a principle may be open to challenge in the physical realm, it seems to be the fundamental grounding and organizing principle for archetypes in the human realm. Again, Ogilvy (1977) seems to have captured this insight best: "The body is not just a model, not simply good

Figure 8. The Structures of Archetypes:
Each Is Contained Within All.

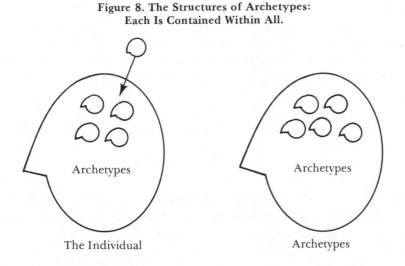

simile for the self. It *is* in one sense *one* of the selves. . . . In another sense it contains all the selves within it and serves as a mirror testifying to conflicts among those other selves as a mirror testifying to whether conflicts among those other selves are being dealt with or denied. In this second sense the body serves also as a model for all the other selves which also, like Anaxagorean spermata or Leibnitzian monads or Jungian archetypes, contain all other selves within themselves as seen from a slightly different perspective" (p. 118). Jung put it this way: "In the unconscious the individual archetypes are not insulated from one another, but are in a state of contamination, of complete mutual interpenetration and fusion. [Often it is] a well-nigh hopeless undertaking to tear a single archetype out of the living tissue of the psyche; but despite their interwovenness they do form units of meaning that can be apprehended intuitively" (quoted in Jacobi, 1959, pp. 65–66).

Conclusion

The discussion in this chapter makes it highly tempting, and thereby all the more dangerously false, to consider one characteristic kind or level of stakeholders, as somehow more "real" than all the others. For instance, it is natural to infer that

I feel that archetypes are somehow more real or more fundamental than social system actors (see Chapters Two and Three).
This impression, however understandable, is mistaken. I have
stressed the role of archetypal characters in seeking a basis for
explaining the complexity of human behavior only because I
feel that a serious and systematic examination of the influence
of archetypes has not been seriously attempted before in the
theoretical design and management of human systems. I do not,
however, regard one level as more fundamental or more real
than another, with an important exception and qualification to
be discussed in Chapter Ten. Indeed, it is the very failure to regard all levels as equally real and important that in my opinion
has hampered social science in general and management in specific from developing more comprehensive, integrated theories
of human behavior.

Figure 9 shows the various levels of stakeholders we have
considered thus far. The figure has deliberately been arranged in
a straight-line or linear fashion to show the typical conception
of stakeholders, that is, that somehow they are arranged in
strict hierarchical levels.

A truer picture than that shown in Figure 9, however,
would be a circle showing the mutual interpenetration and
interaction of stakeholders at all levels of social reality simultaneously. If archetypes and ego-states are capable of infusing
organizational and institutional structures, of "causing" archaic
impulses to break through the most rationally conceived systems, then it is also true that organizational and institutional
structures are capable of influencing the development of ego-
states and "causing" new archetypal shapes to form (recall the
earlier quotes from Maccoby). *Neither the psychological nor the
sociological is somehow more real or more fundamental than
the other.* If such were the case, then this would be analogous in
physics to saying that the world of everyday objects is somehow
more real than phenomena at the subatomic level or vice versa.
Each is merely the environment and the precondition for the
other.

A number of major social thinkers, among them Parsons
(1970), Slater (1970), and Wrong (1970), have made the point

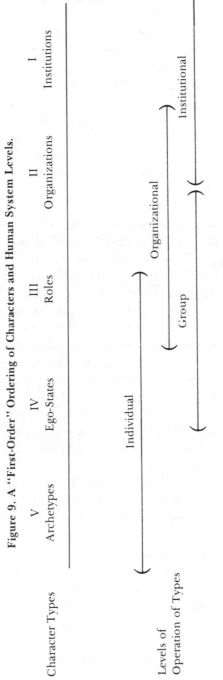

Figure 9. A "First-Order" Ordering of Characters and Human System Levels.

about the mutual interaction and interpenetration between the psychological and sociological: "There does not seem to be any serious doubt that the superego is primarily social and cultural in origin" (Parsons, 1970, p. 68).

Without a doubt one of the most outstanding figures in the field of organization studies is that of James Thompson (1967). Thompson's theory perhaps epitomizes the treatment and conception of organizations in the "rational" sense. His work richly deserves all the credit it has received. It shows us the promise of an organization theory rationally conceived. There is, however, another Thompson, William (1971), whose work, while generally unknown to organization theorists, has special meaning and significance for an alternate conception of organization theory that is more in tune with the concept of archetypes. In his immensely provocative and stimulating book, *At the Edge of History* (1971), William Thompson shows how four archetypal characters, the Hunter or Warrior, the Shaman or Medicine Man, the Clown or Fool, and the Chief, can be construed as the basic building blocks of society and all institutions. Thus, when they are institutionalized and developed further, as they have been in modern society, the Hunter becomes the Military; the Shaman, the Medical profession; the Fool, the Artist and the Entertainment Industry; the Chief, the Manager and Managerial Class. Thompson shows how over time these four basic archetypal characters have become progressively refined and elaborated into the impersonal, institutionalized forms as we now know them. What he does not do is to complete the circle as we have attempted to do in this chapter. That is, do institutions exert influence on the inner personalities of people such as to "cause" new archetypes to emerge, to form, as it were, around the symbols that are in tune with the images of an age? I have argued in effect that the answer is "yes." If this answer is correct, then it promises to shed deeper insight and meaning on the concepts of organizational culture and organizational symbolism. In a word, organizational symbols are symbolic of the complex mixtures of stakeholders, "real" and archetypal, which compose the structure of organizations and the individuals that compose them.

Finally, William Thompson's book causes me to raise the following question. If, as we have seen, archetypes are structured such that each is "contained" in the other in the sense that each archetype is in principle capable of stimulating the operation of all the other archetypes, is the same true of all system stakeholders at all levels? That is, are all system stakeholders somehow (that is, in some fashion) contained in all others? Or, like physics, do stakeholders follow different "laws" at different levels of reality? My belief is that stakeholders at different levels do indeed follow different social laws. This, in part, helps to account for the immense difficulty in explaining human behavior. Note that it is *not* the case that stakeholders at each level do not interpenetrate one another at all other levels. The question is how far, how deeply, do they interpenetrate, influence, and contain one another? One answer is "pretty deeply." If one thing is characteristic of human behavior, it is that any human act seems capable of setting off stakeholders at any and every level simultaneously. As humans, we seem to have an incredible capacity to jump back and forth between the various levels of human reality in the shortest span of times without being aware of it. It is no wonder that human communication is so tortuous.

We have just begun to make an inventory of the characters that so profoundly shape the many selves of our lives. In the next chapter we shall continue our exploration.

CHAPTER SEVEN

How Archetypes Influence Corporate Affairs and Everyday Life

Chapter Six introduced the idea that archetypes constitute the deepest layers of the human mind. As such, archetypes constitute the deepest layers of experience that the human mind is capable of having and the deepest layers of knowledge that the mind is capable of having of and about itself.

Because of the extreme difficulty of grasping the concept of archetypes and of the extreme elusiveness of archetypes themselves, it is important that I present some examples of some current "archetypes in action." This is the purpose of the present chapter.

Because of the extreme mutual interpenetration of archetypes and the extreme overlap between stakeholders at the various levels of social life, one of the main purposes of this chapter is to show how archetypes and stakeholders at all levels intrude themselves into the workings of the most practical and seemingly insignificant activities of everyday life. I have deliberately chosen to emphasize the action of archetypes in human affairs, and, by this deliberate emphasis, I hope to amend the early total neglect of archetypes in social analysis.

If anything, the chapter is testimony to one of the prime properties of archetypes and of social system stakeholders stressed in the previous chapter: their constant if not extreme mutual interpenetration, containment, and interaction. As was emphasized, each archetype is contained in every other archetype. If there is any purpose or reason for this, it is best explained in terms of the concept of compensation.

In the world of everyday life and ordinary logic, we are constantly admonished to keep our categories and our life rational, orderly, and in shape. Things should be in their proper place and order; they should not radically overlap and fall into more than one category lest we lose our senses, that is, our mind, our very ability to reason.

If there is any "rational" reason for the extreme overlap of archetypes, it is to let our mind break out of its stifling and fragmenting traps. In a word, the extreme overlap of archetypes expresses the mind's need to compensate for narrow compartmentalization, to let neglected aspects of our soul communicate to us, to let them have their day in court, so to speak, to be heard. If those repressed aspects of ourselves have to intrude into our nice, neat category systems that were designed to hold them at bay, if they have to mess up our logical schemes, then they will do so if this is the only way they can be heard. Archetypes thus follow a different ordering principle to teach us that there is more than one way to grasp or to contain (that is, order) reality.

If archetypes and social system stakeholders overlap (but not as radically as do archetypes within themselves), then they do so in order to teach us that the human mind and human social systems exist on several different planes of reality simultaneously. That is, human reality can be defined as a manifold conversation between stakeholders at many levels occurring simultaneously. If the concept of reality is holistic and not fragmented, then almost by definition people are forced to deal with reality holistically. As much as they try to contain reality to a single level for their ease and convenience, it nonetheless bursts through all the nice containers and forces itself upon them at all levels all at once. Humanity is not doomed to deal with either the conscious or the unconscious, the psychological or the sociological separately but *both* simultaneously. A human being is the special creature, uniquely created and defined, that exists simultaneously on all levels of reality. In a word, the overlap between stakeholders and archetypes both forces us and enables us to deal with contradictory aspects, components, and elements of reality—of ourselves as whole beings.

Overview

Figure 10 gives an overview of the examples of archetypes in action that shall be discussed briefly in this chapter. As before, the classification must be taken with a "big grain of

Figure 10. An Overview of Some Archetypes in Action.

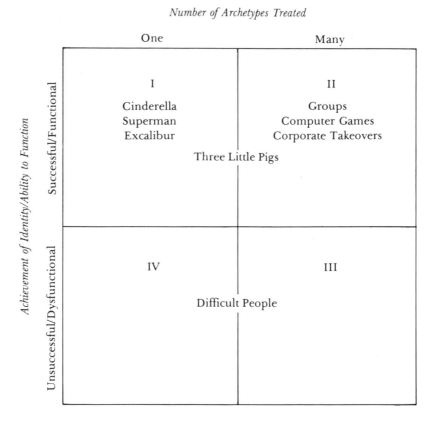

salt." As I have stressed constantly, when one is dealing with a concept such as archetypes, there is a tremendous dynamism to their properties. Indeed, extreme dynamism is one of their chief defining properties.

Figure 10 indicates that, for broad, rough purposes of classification, the examples that portray archetypes can be classified along two dimensions. The first has to do with the basic number of archetypes that are treated in a particular motif. As we shall see, one of the characteristic differences between treatments is whether they deal in depth with a single archetype or with many and whether they deal with a small or large social system. The second dimension has to do with the idea, however expressed, of whether or not the struggle or the quest for identity, health, well-being, and individuation is successful. The themes here are many and varied. They can refer to whether one's degree of integration is successful or functional within oneself or the group or whether it is unsuccessful or dysfunctional.

Cell I refers to those examples or stories of archetypes that typically treat a single archetype in depth and in which the quest for identity is successful. In a word, the archetype successfully achieves personal or individual control and/or identity. He or she has successfully met and overcome the challenges of the world. Cell IV also tends to treat single, individual archetypes in depth but the achievement of control and/or identity is unsuccessful or only partially successful.

Cells II and III, however, typically treat a collection, a set, or a system of archetypes. The properties of any single archetype are defined or contrasted in terms of the others. Where cell III represents the achievement of successful societal or social order/identity, cell IV does not.

It must be stressed again that there is a tremendous degree of overlap and movement between the cells. It is the nature of an archetype that it is constantly doing battle with the characteristic struggles and opportunities of each cell. Just when an archetype is at the lowest ebb of its success, the world can turn suddenly and it can find itself at the highest. Indeed, it is only by "first" experiencing the dangers, fears, frustrations, and trauma of the depths of despair, that it can rise to the top. Conversely, it is just when it is safely implanted at the top that it can sink swiftly to the bottom. One begins to form an appreciation of why one of the major archetypes of the Tarot cards is the Wheel of Fortune, with its sharply reversing, continually recurring, cycle of ups and downs. By the same token, the line of separation between an individual archetype and a group of archetypes is exceedingly thin by virtue of the principle that each archetype is contained within all and/or each. With these qualifications and reservations in mind, I shall proceed by discussing each example. Each cell should be thought of as containing those aspects of every archetype that are found within that particular cell. Finally, with a few exceptions, I shall proceed by discussing each cell in turn. A major exception is the first example, computer games. The reason for this departure, as we shall see shortly, is one of the most striking features of archetypes: their ability to burst forth in the seemingly most unexpected places at the most unexpected times.

Computer Games: The Wizardry Phenomenon

Like many adults, I have never taken the recent phenomenon of computer video games with any great seriousness. Because of the nature of my own personality, I tend not to be interested in games whose structure is fixed or for which there is a single correct solution, even though a great deal of skill may be involved in attaining a winning score. Frankly, I find such games rather boring. However, in the course of writing this book, I became primed to see some of the games in a rather different light.

This came about because I own an Apple computer. As a result, I receive various computer publications that have a tie-in with the Apple corporation. While I was browsing through recent issues of the computer magazine *Softline,* it suddenly hit me that one of the most powerful examples of archetypes in action had been there all along, right in front of my eyes.

Over the last few years, a whole series of computer games has evolved that allows players to test their skills in competition against a set of formidable opponents, that is, the characters

that compose the games. The ads for these "games" make perfectly and abundantly clear the archetypal nature of the opponents that are built into these games. The ads portray, in the
slickest and glossiest of terms (that is, through artwork), the most
diverse pantheon of mythological characters that one can do
battle against. Not only are there mythological characters—
minotaurs and half human–half animal creatures—but the men
and the women that appear in the games are themselves larger
than life in their every physical feature. They make the characters in the recent movie *Conan the Barbarian* look tame by comparison.

Irony of ironies: The computer, perhaps *the* modern
archetype of impersonal, cold, calculating science and technology, has itself become the projective dumping ground of humanity's inner psyche. This conclusion becomes all the more
striking and powerful when one realizes that one has very little
reason to think that the designers of these games had any conscious appreciation of the fact that they were engaged in pro-
jecting their internal archetypes onto their games.

One of the best if not most striking examples of these
games is that of *Wizardry*. A recent article in *Softline* puts it as
follows: "*Wizardry* is a game apart from others of its genre. Its
success probably rests on its unique abilities: No other game
allows as much flexibility in building your own characters,
designating strengths and weaknesses that have clear effects;
more important, no other game allows you to take groups of
characters, up to six at a time, into [a] dungeon, where they
interact and work together to overcome monsters and obstacles.
Characters can trade gold and equipment freely, cast beneficial
spells on each other, and change position in the expedition to
benefit all. Or they can all run from monsters; if one runs, all
run" (Milich, 1982, p. 38).

Robert Woodhead, one of the designers of the game and
one of the very few who have a background in psychology and
hence some insight into the popularity of his own creation, freely acknowledges that *Wizardry* is a "projective game." That is,
"people tend to put their personalities on the characters they
invent":

The world of *Wizardry* can be populated with characters of different races—dwarf, elf, gnome, hobbit, and human—and different classes, starting as mages [sorcerers], priests, fighters, or thieves; characters can earn the right to become samurai, bishops [a combination of priest and sorcerer, or mage], ninjas [evil inhuman fighting machines], and lords [a combination of samurai and priest]. The dungeon has ten levels to conquer and there are numerous personal levels through which your characters progress as they gain experience and strengthen their attributes. [A character has a combination of six basic attributes at various levels: (1) strength, which affects one's ability in combat; (2) and (3) I.Q. and piety, which affect one's ability to cast spells; (4) vitality, which affects the amount of damage one can sustain before dying; (5) agility, which determines the order in which attacks on a character will happen; and (6) luck, which as writers of the *Wizardry* manual put it, "helps in many mysterious ways."] You can create as many as twenty characters per [computer program], any six of which you can gather in the tavern to send on expedition into the maze. Together your band fights monsters, searches for treasure, or has a good old time at the inn [Milich, 1982, p. 38].

As those who have played *Wizardry* testify in their own words, it is more than "just a game." The characters one creates are a part of one's self. Hence, when one of the characters dies, it is like having a part of oneself die as well. Verbatim quotes from those who have played the game are immensely revealing of the hold that such "games" have on the psyche: "It sure helps to relax a person after a hard day at work. That troll does look like my boss"; "Sometimes I submerge myself into my characters, I lose almost all sense of my own identity. I once played for three days straight without coming up out of the game. When my party was finally devastated, I almost broke down into tears"; "I'd liken *Wizardry* to a fantasized system of personnel management. As the manager of a small group of individuals . . . you must manipulate the members' performance against the 'competition' so that they achieve a certain goal. In *Wizardry,* as in real life, the goal can be mere survival, or the quest for power, or, over the long haul, the pot of gold" (Adams, 1982, pp. 31-32).

Perhaps the most interesting and potentially important

use of such games has been in the field of child psychotherapy. As is well known, an accepted psychotherapeutic technique of working with children, who can not verbalize their inner states as well as adults can, is that of play therapy. What children play with and how they do so offers a window into their inner processes. Thus, for instance, if a certain doll represents a parent and it is treated in a rough manner, then one gets from the child a glimpse of what is going on inside the child in relation to a parent. Because *Wizardry* allows one to create a number of characters and to project onto them characteristics in which one may be deficient, one has the opportunity to observe the psychological issues one is wrestling with. It should be noted that this holds no less true with adults than it does with children.

Again, how ironic that a machine that has come to symbolize the very epitome of humanity's impersonal, calculating abilities carried to the highest levels of scientific and technological development should come to serve as a prime vehicle for allowing a person to observe his or her own psyche. It seems no matter what humanity attempts, it is doomed to observe its own archetypal nature staring back at it. Archetypes are not dead, as by definition they could never be. They just crop up in the strangest of places. They are alive—whether they are "well" is another matter—and functioning on the computer. However, if this is the case, then it explains all too well the deep fascination and appeal such "games" have for "kids" of all ages. No wonder it is so easy to get hooked on video and computer games. The addicting quality is within all of us. As a result, it is impossible, in the extreme, to ban all such games. They will merely come back in another form. Indeed, if there is a serious and legitimate debate that deserves to be held, it should be over which *forms* of archetypes are acceptable to us as a society, not their ultimate restriction. If the games are archetypal, then total restriction is a mortal impossibility. Even more fundamental is the question of responsibility. Who or what is responsible for the design of archetypes on computers?

If, as I firmly believe, archetypes have made a new and fundamental link with the computer, then one can make some important, if not potentially disturbing, social predictions. One of the most significant occurrences, I believe, is the inevitable intrusion of archetypal games into the large theme parks, for example, Disneyland. It is only a small step from archetypes contained inside a computer program and projected onto a TV screen to rides (better yet, "experiences") wherein one can play with archetypes in the form of robots. The technology that is capable of doing one can ultimately do the other. Whether "because it can be done it should be done" is, of course, another matter.

Even potentially more significant, disturbing, and promising all at once is the inevitable marriage of archetypes with computer information systems. There is little doubt that for most people computers are puzzling, frightening, intriguing, hypnotic, and so forth. There is also little doubt that one of the least explored and yet most powerful aspects of information is archetypal. Advertisers understand this only too well even if the current designers of management information systems do not. So also do politicians, campaign designers, and TV producers. The most powerful kind of information is that which is embedded in a character with which we instinctively ally ourselves, in which we put our deepest trust. It is only time before this finally occurs to the designers of computer systems. In the language of Chapter Four, most computer information systems have been designed by ST minds for other ST minds. The whole notion of NF information systems for NF minds is virtually unexplored. It constitutes one of the greatest and potentially most frightening revolutions in the history of human design efforts.

Archetypes Go to the Movies

In many ways the title of this section is a misnomer, for archetypes have always been at the basis of movies. By definition, there is an archetypal basis to any story that has a deep appeal or hold on the mind. For an extensive, in-depth analysis of the basic (read "archetypal") "stories" of Western culture, the reader is referred to the brilliant analysis by Northrop Frye, *Anatomy of Criticism* (1973).

By the phrase "archetypes go to the movies" I mean a particular archetype, one that is the heart of a large number of contemporary movies. This is the archetypal myth of the hero. This archetype is so predominantly featured in the current rash of movies that it would be almost impossible to list them all. A few of the ones that come most easily to mind are *Clash of the Titans, Excalibur, Star Trek, Star Wars,* and *Superman.* In every case there is a central figure who typifies the primary features of the "myth or story of the hero." Indeed, this myth is one of the most stylized archetypes to which one can point.

The hero is typically born under miraculous or extraordinary conditions. Superman, for example, is born on another planet; he is not of this world. The hero is thus set apart from ordinary mortals right from "the very beginning." He is destined to take on special tasks, to lead, and to set special examples. The tasks he undertakes are designed both to test and to prepare him for his special assignments and/or role later in life.

While the hero is usually born under special circumstances and thus is not "one of the people," he typically spends the first or early part of his life among the people and is not recognized as different from them except to a very few (again, witness Superman, especially *Superman I*). In this phase of his life the hero is "one of them." This juxtaposition of contradictory qualities is, as we have seen in the previous chapter, one of the prime features of archetypes. The hero is and is not—*at the same time*—one of the people.

Around the early onset of manhood, the hero receives a sign or a call that the time has come for him to separate himself from ordinary mortals. He must undertake a long and difficult journey "to find out finally who he is and just what he is destined to be." This difficult journey is designed (1) to make final the break between him and ordinary mortals, (2) to test him, to ensure that he is really worthy, and (3) to humble him, to show him that even heroes (Superman) have their limitations, their fatal flaws. (No single archetype is totally complete or perfect within itself, *even though there are archetypes that* stand for *"perfection" and "completeness."* An archetype may stand for perfection but it is not perfection itself.) Such arduous tests are necessary if people are to learn the difficult lesson that perfection is something that is attained only by the gods, not by ordinary mortals, perhaps not even by superheroes.

In some tales of the hero, this part of the hero's development is fraught with overcoming the most horrible mythological beasts and monsters. (A good example is *Clash of the Titans.*)
The hero's struggles symbolize the difficulties humans face in
developing to maturity and independence: There are psychic
pitfalls at every twist and turn.

If the hero overcomes the obstacles and becomes what
he was destined to be, then another—and perhaps the most difficult—part of his journey begins. This is the journey home, the
return back to the world of ordinary life. It is not necessarily the
return home per se that is difficult but the feat of attempting to
convince others—who have not taken his journey, who have not
seen and who have not done what he has—to believe in all he
has witnessed and experienced. In many ways this is the story
of the creative inventor—he who has seen a new vision of what
"might be," not "what is," and is faced with the tremendous
obstacles and frustrations of conveying his strange, terrible, and
bewildering images to those who lack his powers of imagination.
To achieve his new insights, he must deliberately separate himself from the ordinary ways of seeing and of doing. But to effect change, he must reconnect himself with society and attempt
to convince those who have not "seen" what he has of the truth
of his visions—no mean or small feat! Little wonder that such a
creature is labeled a hero! If he succeeds, he not only stands to
become recognized as a great leader, but he achieves something
even more precious: completion of his psychological development as a whole, integrated human being—as close to a god as a
mortal can come.

Neumann (1970) has given a psychoanalytic interpretation of the myth of the hero by determining just who or what is
the beast (most typically a dragon) that the hero is attempting
to slay. For Neumann, the myth of the hero is a psychoanalytic
fable of the perils of achieving selfhood, that is, an integrated
personality:

> The tests of masculinity and the proofs of ego stability,
> will, power, bravery, knowledge of "heaven," and so forth,
> which are demanded of the hero, have their historical equiva-
> lents in the rites of puberty. Just as the problem of the First
> Parents is resolved in the [story or myth of] the dragon fight,

and, in turn, succeeded by the hero's encounter with woman as his partner and his soul, so, through the initiation ceremony, the neophyte is detached from the parental sphere, and becomes a marriageable young man capable of founding a family. But what happens in myth and in history also happens in the individual and on the basis of archetypal determinism. The central feature of puberty psychology is [revealed in] the syndrome of the dragon fight. . . . The personal aspects of this situation, a small part of which has been formulated psychoanalytically as the personalistic Oedipus complex, are merely surface aspects of the conflict with the First Parents, i.e., with the parental archetypes. And in this process [the person] has to "kill the parents" [or slay the dragon to achieve selfhood or autonomy] [1970, p. 205].

Wilber (1981b) offers another psychoanalytic view: "The slain monster is the Great Mother, or one of her symbols, or one of her consorts. And the treasure 'hard to attain' that the serpent monster guards and tries to conceal is simply the ego structure itself. This is significant, for the serpent is really the uroboros, the structure which, with the Great Mother, kept the ego immersed and encoiled in unconsciousness. The dragon guards the ego—and that's what the hero must liberate. Prior to this time in history [when the hero myth first emerges, ca. 2500 B.C.], the Great Mother . . . sacrificially swallowed up egos and returned them to herself in subconsciousness, thereby preventing . . . the necessary emergence of egoic consciousness. But sometime during this [historical] period, the hero clutched his egoic self out of the jaws of the Devouring Mother and secured his own emancipation" (p. 184).

Since every individual and every generation has to fight this battle—for every person it is a first time—little wonder that the myth or story of the hero is endlessly recurring. It merely changes its form to suit the times. For one age it is Jesus; for another, it is an E.T. (extraterrestrial being); it is a character who brings love to life and is brought back to life by love.

Fairy Tales: "Cinderella," "The Three Little Pigs"

Some stories do not change or change very little. They have an almost timeless appeal and quality. Bruno Bettelheim's,

The Uses of Enchantment (1977), is a masterful analysis of the appeal that fairy tales have. It is his contention that fairy tales not only help the child to develop psychologically by representing in a form the child can comprehend emotionally (that is, unconsciously) the problems with which he or she is struggling, but that the themes of fairy tales portray the detailed phases of emotional development through which the child must proceed if he or she is to grow normally. A classic in this regard is the story of Cinderella:

> "Cinderella" sets forth the steps in personality development required to reach self-fulfillment, and presents them in fairy-tale fashion so that every person can understand what is required of him to become a full human being. This is hardly surprising, since the fairy tale, as I have tried to show throughout this book, represents extremely well the workings of our psyche: what our psychological problems are, and how these can best be mastered. Erikson, in his model of the human life-cycle, suggests that the ideal human being develops through what he calls "phase-specific psychosocial crises" if he achieves the ideal goals of each phase in succession. These crises in their sequence are: First, basic trust—represented by Cinderella's experience with the original good mother, and what this firmly implanted in her personality. Second, autonomy—as Cinderella accepts her unique role and makes the best of it. Third, initiative—Cinderella develops this as she plants the twig and makes it grow with the expression of her personal feelings, tears, and prayers. Fourth, industry—represented by Cinderella's hard labors, such as sorting out the lentils. Fifth, identity—Cinderella escapes from the ball, hides in the dovecote and tree, and insists that the prince see and accept her in her negative identity as "Cinderella" before she assumes her positive identity as his bride, because any true identity has its negative as well as its positive aspects. According to Erikson's scheme, having ideally solved these psychosocial crises by having achieved the personality attributes just enumerated, one becomes ready for true intimacy with the other [Bettelheim, 1977, p. 275].

If "Cinderella" is a story that speaks more to individual personality development—the obstacles and the stages that are a part of becoming an adult—then the story of "The Three Little Pigs" speaks as directly to the concerns of the adult as it does to those of the child. In these days when Westerners are inclined to turn to the stories of the East for inspiration and life renewal, we would do well to remember, if not relearn, that there are stories in our own tradition and culture that speak directly to the concerns of our everyday, adult lives. Indeed, the story of "The Three Little Pigs" can be read as a story about strategic planning. Why is it that I often feel that somehow our best analysts of the mind have appreciated this better than our best policy analysts? I quote from Bettelheim:

> The myth of Hercules deals with the choice between following the pleasure principle or the reality principle in life. So, likewise, does the fairy story of "The Three Little Pigs."
>
> Stories like "The Three Little Pigs" are much favored by children over all "realistic" tales, particularly if they are presented with feeling by the storyteller. Children are enraptured when the huffing and puffing of the wolf at the pig's door is acted out for them. "The Three Little Pigs" teaches the nursery-age child in a most enjoyable and dramatic form that we must not be lazy and take things easy, for if we do, we may perish. Intelligent planning and foresight combined with hard labor will make us victorious over even our most ferocious enemy—the wolf! The story also shows the advantages of growing up, since the third and wisest pig is usually depicted as the biggest and oldest.
>
> The houses the three pigs build are symbolic of man's progress in history: from a lean-to shack to a wooden house, finally to a house of solid brick. Internally, the pigs' actions show progress from the id-dominated personality to the superego-influenced but essentially ego-controlled personality.
>
> The littlest pig builds his house with the least care out of straw; the second uses sticks; both throw their shelters together as quickly and effortlessly as they can, so they can play for the rest of the day. Living in accordance with the pleasure principle, the younger pigs seek immediate gratification, without a thought for the future and the dangers of reality, although the middle pig shows some growth in trying to build a somewhat more substantial house than the youngest.
>
> Only the third and oldest pig has learned to behave in accordance with the reality principle; he is able to postpone his desire to play, and instead acts in line with his ability to foresee what may happen in the future. He is even able to predict correctly the behavior of the wolf—the enemy, or stranger within,

which tries to seduce and trap us; and therefore the third pig is able to defeat powers both stronger and more ferocious than he is [competition?]. The wild and destructive wolf stands for all asocial, unconscious, devouring powers against which one must learn to protect oneself, and which one can defeat through the strength of one's ego [1977, pp. 41–42].

If Bettelheim is not talking about strategic and business planning as much as fairy tales, then perhaps I am missing the point. I do not think I am.

Groups: Types and Archetypes

It is beyond the scope of a single chapter to demonstrate in detail that all of the aforementioned processes that operate in the individual also operate in small groups and in organizations (Berne, 1966). As we advance up the scale or levels of human phenomena from the single individual to that of the organization, there is a difference in degree, but not in kind, in the explanation of human behavior. Characters, both real and imagined, actual and symbolic, develop in small groups. Groups develop myths and stories no less than individuals do to give meaning to their existence and structure to their relationships. As individuals develop their character structure through such mechanisms as identification, introjection, and projection, groups also utilize these very same mechanisms. Groups, like individuals, develop split characters to handle the split feelings of goodness and badness with which they must deal. I quote from a recent volume on groups (Gibbard, Hartman, and Mann, 1978):

The group situation recreates the basic nuclear-family conditions that spawn the Oedipus complex. The leader is regarded as father, and some female member or the female subgroup or the group-as-a-whole is regarded as the mother (assuming the leader is male). . . .
One additional view of the small group has provocative, but largely unexplored, developmental implications—the notion that the group is unconsciously experienced as a maternal entity. Bion, Durkin, Gibbard and Hartman, Jaques, Ruiz, and

Scheidlinger see the group as a preoedipal mother. Slater, too, adopts this point of view, as it relates to boundary evolution [p. 8].

In small groups there is an effort to split good and bad and to put the good into the group and the bad into the leader or disorganizing subgroup. This effort culminates in the revolt against the leader. There is an attempt to force him in the group fully on the group's terms (make him good) or to exclude him fully by destroying him. The revolt is preceded by the expression of several components of distress. Whatever the antecedents, there is an effort to get back into the group anyone or anything (symbols, ideas) experienced as good. This situation occurs because members may at the same time have projected onto the leader good, "ideal" qualities which are then recaptured and introjected during the revolt. Although the leader is ostensibly excluded in the revolt, he is simultaneously included by the mechanisms of introjection [p. 173].

Groups are replete with mythological and myth-like assumptions about themselves. Members and leaders make use of conscious fantasy productions, involve their fellows in issues of political faith and ideology, have rituals and ritualistic activity, and invent religious-like beliefs as well [p. 274].

Corporate Takeovers

If the metaphors and dizzying images of the preceding chapter and in this chapter thus far have left the reader asking, "But what has this *really* got to do with the 'real' world?," then the examples in this and the next section should help. Where some of our previous examples have hinted at a possible point of connection with the business world, the next two examples relate directly.

In an article that can be considered nothing other than utterly fascinating, "Ambushes, Shootouts, and Knights of the Round Table: The Language of Corporate Takeovers," Paul Hirsch (1983) convincingly demonstrates that when one large business attempts to take over another, the language in which it is conducted is anything but subdued. It reflects all the emotions, fears, and joys that one should expect to find when the spoils of winning and of losing are so big. In the terms of this book, when one is in a situation that is so rife with potential uncer-

tainty, exhilaration, conflict, and hard feelings, one should expect to see archetypal imagery being used to cope with the intensity of the feelings being expressed and to attempt to contain them. As Hirsch himself points out, this is indeed one of
the fundamental purposes of the language that is used. It helps
to insulate both parties, taker and takee, from the intensity of
their feelings.

The gist of Hirsch's findings is best presented in a brief,
summary paragraph. I quote:

The takeover event in itself clearly conforms to a predict-
able set of scenarios or scripts. In the most neutral terms, this
boils down to offer $\longrightarrow$ decisions/actions taken $\longrightarrow$ outcome. In
the business world, this relatively simple diagram has taken on
the far more colorful forms available from such well known
popular genres as the western (ambush and shootout replace
[the more bland terms] offer and actions taken), the love affair
and/or marriage, warfare (replete with sieges, barricades, flak,
and soldierly honor),* mystery, and piracy on the high seas
(with raiders and safe harbors). Generic formulations also entail
the frequent appearance of mercenaries or hired guns (investment houses to whom most of the negotiating is delegated), and
black and white knights (culled from tales of chivalry in which
the distressed damsel is either undone or rescued). In virtually
all formulations, the acquiring executive is macho and the target
company [that is, the company to be acquired] is accorded the
female gender ("sleeping beauty" or a bride brought to the
altar; reference to rape also is not uncommon) [Hirsch, 1983, p.
236].

Difficult People—Difficult Archetypes

Who among us has not had the nerve-wracking experience
of giving an oral presentation, which requires considerable effort and time to prepare, and hence has had enough anxiety
connected with it before it is even given? But this is only the be-

---

*Thus Hirsch writes: "For example, the efforts of American Ex-
press to acquire McGraw-Hill were said by many to test the limits of the
normative boundaries for legitimate acquisition tactics: the appropriate
genre here, for coding purposes, became all-out warfare" (1983, p. 237).

ginning. In what seems to be only a few seconds into your presentation, the class or the office terror—whomever—may suddenly burst out, "That's the dumbest idea I've ever heard; do we have to waste our time listening to this junk?" As your stomach convulses and your mind and body wish you had never been born, you panic. You attempt to find *something* to do, to say. What *do* you do? If it took only a microsecond to get you into this pit, it seems to be taking an eternity for you to think of something—anything—to get out of it.

If this situation sounds familiar, it is because it is not rare. The particular situation is just one of a class that has been aptly identified by an organizational consultant, Robert Bramson (1981). In his years of travels around organizations, Bramson found that the same kinds of difficult people appeared constantly. They appeared with such regularity that he was able to give them short, extremely provocative, but highly identifying names and phrases. In other words, he was dealing with a widely appearing set of characters.

Bramson also found that in every organization there was at least one person who knew how to deal or cope with these difficult people. The word *cope* is extremely important and was chosen with great deliberate care by Bramson. The underlying psychology of "difficult people" is such that they can neither be changed nor dealt with by surface appeals to niceness or to rationality. Such tactics just do not work with them. In this sense, there is a bit of sociopathic behavior to their makeup. Their behavior can only be, at best, contained, blocked, or blunted by very carefully selecting the appropriate psychological strategy. In very few cases is the appropriate strategy that of a direct power confrontation. In fact, this usually fails since one of the primary characteristics of a few of the types is their masterly use of power. Hence, direct confrontation is a game on their turf, and one that will usually ensure their victory.

The names of the types are highly revealing and informative, if not descriptive in themselves. First there is a trio of hostile-aggressives as Bramson calls them: (1) Sherman Tanks, (2) Snipers, and (3) Exploders. Next we find (4) the Compleat Complainer, (5) the Clam, (6) Super-Agreeables and Other Nice

People, (7) Wet Blankets or Negativists, (8) Bulldozers and Balloons—the Know-It-All Experts, and (9) Indecisive Stallers.

We have already met the Sherman Tank in the opening paragraphs of this section. The Sherman Tanks are exactly what the name implies. They attack directly and attempt to run over you, so to speak. There is nothing clean or subtle about them. The intent is to flatten the opponent, who includes just about everyone.

The Sniper is a much more subtle adversary but one who is just as worthy. He or she never or rarely attacks directly. The modus operandi is more one of indirect implication and subtle innuendo. One is never quite sure with a Sniper whether he or she is really attacking. But that is one of their prime characteristics. They want it both ways. They want to and they do not want to attack.

The Clam is another frustrating species of difficult person. One could literally explode a bomb next to them and you would not get a response out of them. Nothing seems to provoke a response from them. If the varieties of the hostile-aggressives have "learned" to attack, then the Clam has learned to protect him- or herself by avoiding all confrontation.

It is beyond the scope of this book to review in any depth the defining characteristics of such people, some of the successful strategies for coping with them, and the underlying psychological forces responsible for producing their behavior. It is, however, instructive to quote from Bramson:

> For some children [the] parental aura of certainty about what is, and what is to come, represents security in a world that often feels unfathomable and inconsistent. For these children, the motivation to acquire facts and to develop orderly frameworks in which to fit those facts is particularly strong. The lesson for them is: Know for sure what the facts are; know for sure how they fit together—then, and only then, can you feel secure.
>
> It is in this way that people are inclined, sometimes driven, to become experts, and what a constructive response to a wish for security it is. The problem for all would-be experts is that much of the world is very hard to nail down. "Facts" are perceived differently by different people [see Chapters Two

and Three]. Opinions about what those facts mean vary even more. In the face of this pervasive ambiguity, some of us abandon any efforts to systematize our perceptions and simply respond to whatever turns up next. Others haven't abandoned these efforts, but have learned to live with or even enjoy ambiguity and the seeming tentativeness of all knowledge. Still others, those Difficult People . . . , just can't stand such uncertainty and strive even harder to impose their own order on everything they can. Their certainty that their theories, facts, and procedures *are* correct makes sane a world otherwise too unpredictable to contemplate.

The basis of a Bulldozer's stability is that tightly held knowledge which, given a changing world, constitutes the only bedrock available. It is therefore not surprising that an attack on the accuracy of that knowledge bites deep. It strikes not only at substantive matter under discussion, but also at deepest levels of personal motivation. Thus, when the plan goes awry, the first line of defense is the ineptitude of others. When that line does not hold, and the cracks in that wall of logic must be faced, the emotional impact can be catastrophic.

Complainers and Negativists . . . feel that the forces that affect their lives are largely out of their control. Bulldozers are the opposite. *Their* early life experiences led to their construction of a world in which they always got what they deserved. Unequivocal praise or blame from parents plus a sense of their own ability to affect things by careful planning and follow-through led easily to the belief that if good or bad things happen, they, not fate or luck, are the cause.

Given such strong needs to feel sure of their own notions of reality and to depend upon their own efforts, small wonder that Bulldozers spurn the ideas and conclusions of others. And each time the Bulldozer clings firmly and methodically to a planned objective, the security that comes from being self-directing, self-sustaining, and unneedful of others is reinforced [1981, pp. 117-119].

Conclusion

This chapter has attempted to demonstrate that archetypes are all around us. They are perennially alive and functioning in every sphere of a person's existence. Once we are sensitized to their existence, we can begin to see them with relative ease.

A deeper and less obvious purpose of this chapter has been to demonstrate that there is an amazing degree of similarity, at the least strong points of contact, between seemingly diverse systems of archetypes. If anything, we need many more studies of archetypes in action.

A recent book by Deal and Kennedy, *Corporate Cultures: The Rites and Rituals of Corporate Life* (1982a), attests to the importance of the study of archetypes both in theory (Chapter Five) and in action (Chapter Six). Although their notion of characters and the range with which they deal are much more limited than those explored in this chapter, Deal and Kennedy show that the concept of an organization's "culture" can be explained in terms of the types of characters present in an organization and the system of interactions that takes place between them. This is important because the concept of organization culture is a sticky and elusive one. Indeed, there may be no more stickier concept in the field of organization studies than that of the culture of an organization. To be sure, an organization's culture is composed of many things: (1) the "rules," written and unwritten, of the organization's game, that is, who gets ahead and why, what it takes to succeed "around here"; (2) its special language and dictionaries of terms; (3) its jokes, (4) history; (5) myths; (6) rituals; (7) special awards and rewards; (8) ceremonies; and (9) symbols. All these, to be sure, compose an organization's culture. At the same time, it is also true that at the deepest levels, an organization's culture is made up by the special set of characters it consciously and unconsciously selects to represent "it." For instance, one "knows" a lot about an organization if it tends to select predominantly Sherman Tanks.

This chapter also shows why it is so difficult to understand human behavior, singly or in organizations. We know so little about how archetypal characters interact and react across several levels of reality simultaneously. To say more about this is the topic of Chapter Nine. The key question there is, "What is an appropriate philosophy or method of inquiry for studying and knowing more about archetypes?" As we shall show, our methods for obtaining knowledge are themselves founded on various archetypal notions.

CHAPTER EIGHT

Insights from
Organizational Stories

Story . . . is a method. It is an ancient and altogether human method. The human being alone among creatures on the earth is a storytelling animal: sees the present rising out of a past, heading into a future; perceives reality in narrative form.

During every high tide of rationalism—a phenomenon as recurrent in its way as the rising of the oceans—story is not a highly valued method. In the rationalistic periods, the human subject is self-effacing. What counts is not the experience which occasioned insight, nor the moment . . . of conversion, nor the altogether individual, unique, and contingent details of autobiographical narrative; no, what counts in the rationalistic self-image, is that the mind be conformed (1) to *universal* principles, (2) to *general* rules of evidence, and (3) to *clear* and *distinct* concepts accessible to any inquiring and adequately disciplined mind. As a method, story runs against the grain of these criteria. Elements of the universal, the general, and even of the clear and the distinct figure in almost all stories. But whereas in a story these elements are recessive and implicit, in a more rationalistic method they are salient, explicit, ruthlessly dominant. Elements of story are an embarrassment to a fully rationalistic period; rationalism attempts to "demythologize." When encountered in undigested form, not fully imagined, not utterly concrete, not thoroughly experiential, elements of the universal, the general, and the conceptual are an embarrassment to a good story [Novak, 1975, pp. 175-176].

The characters or, as I have called them, the "stakehold-ers," that inhabit social psychological life do not exist as sepa-rate, isolated entities. They exist as part of a complex psycho-social fabric that somehow ties the individual characters together and gives them individual and collective meaning. One of the most powerful integrating mechanisms are stories. The notion of a story is exceedingly appropriate for a book of this kind. If anything is characteristic of stories, it is the fact that they pos-sess at least three essential ingredients: (1) characters, (2) narra-tion, and (3) plot. The characters are generally the "who" part of a story that the narrative, or the "what" part, of the story happens to. The plot is the "why" part, that is, why the narra-tive (the what) happens to the characters (the who). As we shall see, this is not to say that there is always a clear dividing line be-tween the three aspects. Indeed, it is precisely the fact that it is often extremely difficult to disentangle the properties of the characters from one another or from the narrative or the plot that makes the concept of stories so central to our discussion. The properties of stakeholders do not exist entirely apart from the stories in which they function.

With some important exceptions this chapter does not discuss any stories in detail. In particular, its purpose is not to discuss the general types of stories, their structural characteris-tics or thematic features, that are representative of the basic motifs of Western civilization. Fortunately for us this has al-ready been superbly done by Frye (1973). Instead, the purpose of this chapter is to contrast three distinct forms of storytelling as they pertain to the central theme of this book, understanding complex human systems.

As a result, scientific theorizing as a very special form of storytelling is described. In its own characteristic way science does tell stories, even though this is not generally recognized as such. Since the stories of science have a very definite form and structure, they can therefore be contrasted with other kinds of storytelling. The form of science's stories is thus compared with archetypal stories and with a kind that is intermediate between the two. The purpose of this comparison is to show what is in-volved in going or translating between the forms of knowledge that are contained in three very different approaches to social knowledge. The comparison is also intended to show that conventional science is far from being the only valid way of expressing knowledge about the psychosocial world in a form that is appropriate for motivating action.

The General Form of Scientific Stories

One way of summarizing the argument thus far in this book is as follows: We have shown that the number of forces (stakeholders plus their attendant assumptions) that the modern designer and manager of complex human systems must consider has grown enormously. People everywhere are now threatened by the real and ever-present danger of being overwhelmed by the sheer number of forces, their complexity, their subtlety, and the extreme coupling between them with which they must deal. How, then, can the modern designer or manager cope with this overwhelming complexity? One way is to examine the assumptions associated with an issue and to boil their number down to the most critical ones via the process suggested in Chapter Two. This process handles the problem of coping with an ever-expanding *number* of forces. It does not, however, cope with the no less critical issue of how one links together important assumptions once they have been identified and prioritized with regard to their importance.

To examine the problem of linking together assumptions, Richard O. Mason and I have recently spent considerable time and effort investigating the applicability of a rather special framework for capturing the structure of complex arguments as it applies to policy making. The results of these studies have been published in detail elsewhere (Mitroff and Mitroff, 1980; Mitroff, Mason, and Barabba, 1983a, 1983b).

Figure 11 shows the framework we have used and, in abstract terms, its translation into the field of policy. The framework is derived from the work of the philosopher of science Stephen Toulmin (Toulmin, 1958; Toulmin, Riecke, and Janik, 1979). We believe it is so powerful that we have used it in actual practice to capture the dynamics and intricate structure of

Figure 11. The Logic of Policy Making.

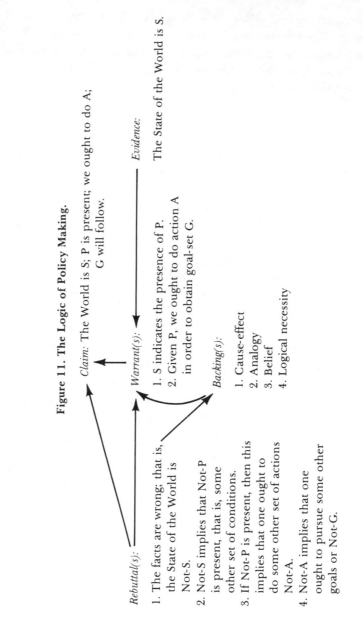

Claim: The World is S; P is present; we ought to do A; G will follow.

Evidence:

The State of the World is S.

Warrant(s):

1. S indicates the presence of P.
2. Given P, we ought to do action A in order to obtain goal-set G.

Backing(s):

1. Cause-effect
2. Analogy
3. Belief
4. Logical necessity

Rebuttal(s):

1. The facts are wrong; that is, the State of the World is Not-S.
2. Not-S implies that Not-P is present, that is, some other set of conditions.
3. If Not-P is present, then this implies that one ought to do some other set of actions Not-A.
4. Not-A implies that one ought to pursue some other goals or Not-G.

an exceedingly complex and important case in public policy making, the 1980 census (Mitroff, Mason, and Barabba, 1983b). The basic notion is that policy making is a process of forming, weighing, and evaluating numerous premises in a complex, continually changing and unfolding argument. The premises in these arguments are in effect the assumptions that are made with regard to the stakeholders that are judged to be relevant to the policy issue under consideration.

Essentially, the framework is an elaboration and expansion on the traditional and classic form of the syllogism, with some very important additions. The Evidence represents the factual base or part of an argument. In general terms, it asserts that "the State of the World" is S. For instance, a typical example is, "For the past six months our average return on investments has been or is 25 percent." The Warrant represents the "if-then" part of an argument, which allows one to "go from" the Evidence to the Claim, the outcome or the conclusion of the argument we are trying to establish. If the Evidence plays the form of the minor premise of an argument (this set of facts is true about this particular organization), then the Warrant plays the role of the major premise (all organizations in this particular situation justify action A to restore them, increase their profits, obtain goals G, and so on). In short, the Warrant is the part of an argument that allows one to justify deriving or supporting the Claim from the Evidence.

Notice that Warrants can become quite complex. For instance, the first Warrant says that "*if* S is observed to be the case, *then* S indicates the presence of some other condition (P) about the particular organization in question." As such, the Warrant, in this case, is an inference. S can be something either about the environment or about the internal organization (for example, strengths, weaknesses). Given that S is the case, it can or may *indicate* the *presence* of some other condition about the organization.

If the Warrant(s) is (are) not accepted on its (their) face value, then the Backing comes into play. The Backing is the set of deeper background reasons whose role is to validate or justify belief in the Warrant. Thus, for instance, the strongest forms of the Backing are "cause-effect" and "logical necessity." Under "cause-effect" one argues, in effect, that, given the truth of the Evidence, the Claim must happen or follow. In other words, the argument is that, given the truth of the Evidence, it is both necessary and sufficient for the occurrence of the Claim. Under "logical necessity" one argues that it is logically inconceivable or impossible that the Claim could fail to occur given the truth of the Evidence.

Given the fact that cause-effect and logical necessity hold only for a simple closed universe, it is logically dubious that cause-effect and logical necessity hold in general for complex social situations. As a result, most Warrants are justified on the basis of analogy and belief. The world in which most managers operate does not justify cause-effect or logical necessity. It is vastly more complicated than this, as the case in Chapter Two shows.

Under analogy, one says that a particular situation is "sufficiently like" some other situation such that what applied or followed from the previous situation applies in this one as well. Under belief, someone who is powerful or credible argues that he or she believes such-and-such to be the case; therefore, the Claim follows.

This is where the real power of the Toulmin framework comes into play. The extreme complexity of policy arguments and the tenuousness of all policy situations renders the use of analogy and belief to be almost indispensable. But this means that very few arguments will be logically airtight, that is, deductively certain beyond all doubt or challenge. As a result, *every* argument in the field of policy making is potentially open to challenge (including *this* very argument), hence the reason for the inclusion of the Rebuttal element in the framework. *The Rebuttal is the set of any and all challenges to any and all parts of an argument.* Thus, one can contest the basic facts, the Evidence. One can assert that one has got the basic facts all wrong. In this case, one asserts that not-S is true; in symbols this is often expressed as $\sim$S. Likewise, one can say that $\sim$S indicates the presence of $\sim$P, that is, $\sim$S $\rightarrow$ $\sim$P. In other words, this means that some alternate state of the world ($\sim$S) indicates the presence of some alternate condition about the organization or $\sim$P. Similarly, $\sim$P suggests some alternate course of action, $\sim$A, that is, $\sim$P → $\sim$A. And finally, $\sim$A suggests some alternate set of goals, $\sim$G, for the organization, that is, $\sim$A → $\sim$G.

To make all this both clearer and more concrete, the drug company case in Chapter Two is shown in Figure 12. Figure 12 shows a form of the argument that must be posited to support the particular policy of raising the price of the drug. As was stressed earlier, the premises in the argument are generally the assumptions that are made with regard to the behavioral properties of the stakeholders. It is important to note that, as it stands, Figure 12 is not the only argument that could be stated to support the policy of raising the price of the drug. It is merely illustrative of the kind of argument that must be made.

Figure 12, in particular, reveals the ideal form of scientific stories. The ideal is, one, an impersonal description of the world ("the State of the World is S"). Two, there is the postulation or presumption of a set of impersonal laws or principles (the Warrants) that permit the justified deduction or support of the Claim (we ought to do A to obtain G) from the Evidence. Three, the deepest and preferred forms of the Backing are cause-effect and logical necessity. In the first case of cause-effect, the argument is that the Warrants are themselves justified (warranted) because they merely reflect "the causal structure of the world." In the second case of logical necessity, the Warrants are justified on the basis of rational thought. To affirm or posit principles other than the particular Warrants (for example, the Rebuttals) is, in effect, to think irrationally. Four, in the ideal scientific story, the various parts of the argument are kept strictly apart. It is insisted that Evidence statements ("is") are very different from Warrants ("if-then" or hypotheticals). Whereas "is" statements can supposedly be verified directly through observation, "if-then" statements can never be fully justified since they are universal type propositions. As such, no finite number of observations can establish their universal validity, hence the need for either one of the two types of Backing to establish their validity.

Thus, in the ideal a scientific story is exceedingly rational in a restrictive sense of the term *rational*. It is an impersonal

Figure 12. The Drug Company Case (Chapter Two).

Claim: Raising the price of the drug is justified (policy decision).

Data:

1. Current surveys show that physicians see our drug quality as high.

2. Past company experience shows that physicians will prescribe drugs within a tolerable price range.

Warrant:

1. The current surveys plus past experience are representative; that is, one is justified in extrapolating from them to the broader set of physicians not included in the sample.

2. Surveys plus past experience indicate that physicians are price-insensitive.

3. Price-insensitivity supports the claim that physicians will prescribe high-quality drugs within a tolerable price range.

Backing: Medical tradition: that is, the first concern of medicine has traditionally been with the health of the patient without regard to cost.

Rebuttals:

1. Counter-Claim: A strong case can be made for lowering the price of the drug.

2. Counter-Data: Surveys show that increasing numbers of physicians are prescribing low-price drugs.

3. Counter-Warrant: Past experience is no longer sufficient to support price increases.

4. Counter-Backing: Medical tradition is changing due to rapidly increasing medical costs.

argument designed to convince an impersonal listener that there is no other outcome that could have occurred and that it could have occurred in no other way. Thus, although there are always Rebuttals to every argument, a good scientific story is one that shows the low plausibility of the R's. Indeed, a good scientific story is one that should not depend at all on a listener. It ought to be so rational in and of itself that it does not even need a listener (Popper, 1972).

Again, it must be stressed that this is the ideal of a theory of complex social systems rationally and scientifically conceived in the traditional sense, at least as that ideal has been articulated in the scientific journals on organizations and social systems up to the present time. That it has been shown to be extremely wanting, if not an abject failure, in every one of its defining conditions by contemporary philosophers of science (Churchman, 1961, 1971) has not been enough to diminish this form of thinking or storytelling as the predominant form in the social scientist's world view. The reason may lie in the fact that this type is the preferred form of storytelling of the kinds of intellectuals that tend to predominate in universities (Carroll, 1978).

Notice carefully that I am not objecting to the Toulmin framework per se as a device for organizing one's thoughts and for pinpointing the weak spots in one's reasoning. If anything, this is the way in which the framework should be used. It should just not be read as *the* literal true story of the world. As the earlier discussion in Chapter Two argued, no single story, no matter how internally consistent or plausible, is the only story that can be told about a complex social system. If there is any single, major defect of traditional science, it has been its failure to appreciate this very "fact." The failure to recognize and to appreciate this may have been, more than anything else, responsible for the failure of social science, until very recently, to develop methods for dealing with multiple stories about the world (Allison, 1971).

Also, it should be pointed out that as originally developed by Toulmin (1958), the framework is not limited to capturing the structure of scientific arguments, that is, science's prevailing conception of a story. Indeed, the framework was originally formulated by Toulmin to capture the structure of moral arguments. It was later extended to capture the forms of reasoning that appear in all professional fields of knowledge (Toulmin, Rieke, and Janik, 1979). Thus, Toulmin's framework and the form of scientific stories are identical. If anything, scientific "stories" are a particular rendering of Toulmin.

In-Between or Ego Stories

In 1929, the Russian folklorist, Vladimir Propp, showed that, despite their seemingly endless variations, the plots of thousands of fairy tales could be reduced to some thirty general forms and seven major characters or role figures. Some fifty years later, continuing in this tradition, Greimas (Broms and Gahmberg, 1980) showed that Propp's categories could be reduced further to just six. That is, according to Greimas (and to Propp), there exists a general syntax of stories. This syntax is embodied in the six categories that every story is supposed to contain. These are: (1) the subject of a story, (2) the object of the story, (3) the sender or force initiating the story, (4) the receiver of the object or outcome of the story, (5) the helper in the story, and (6) the story's adversary.

Henri Broms and Henrik Gahmberg (1980) upon whose work this section is largely based, have done the most to apply the Proppian and Greimasian analysis to business and social system situations. In particular, they have used the recent crisis of the Chrysler corporation to illustrate the power of the Proppian and Greimasian method of analysis. This is particularly important, for the analysis of Broms and Gahmberg was based entirely on so-called factual newspaper and magazine accounts. Now if anything seems clear, it is that the newspaper and magazine writers of the Chrysler crisis saw themselves as writing anything but a fairy tale or an epic story. Nevertheless, the contention of Broms and Gahmberg is that, knowingly or not, intentionally or not, the writers of such articles were writing a story whose form could be analyzed in terms set up by Propp and Greimas. More important still, the written accounts fit the Proppian and Greimasian accounts quite well.

Broms and Gahmberg point out that, at a first glance, the most obvious parts of the Chrysler drama are: (1) the *subject* is Chrysler itself; (2) the *object* is the welfare of Chrysler; (3) the *helpers* are Federal funds, loans, the United Auto Workers; (4) the *adversaries* are General Motors, Ford, foreign auto makers; (5) the *sender* is the American economy in the later 1970s; and (6) the *receiver* is also Chrysler itself. Since, like myself, Broms and Gahmberg are interested in the less obvious meanings of stories, they are inclined to probe for the deeper mythological elements that are inherent in all important stories.

On the surface, the subject of the Chrysler crisis is merely Chrysler itself. However, as Broms and Gahmberg astutely point out, the subject of the Chrysler crisis is really the United States. In particular, the real subject is "the Myth of the Great American Economy." One often reads in the press that the size of the Chrysler Corporation symbolizes its importance to the entire American economy. As Broms and Gahmberg put it, "In the business press Chrysler seems to become the metaphor for the myth of the United States. If it goes down, the United States will suffer—both physically and metaphorically (1980, p. 15)." As a result, it should not be surprising to find that the people that Chrysler's board of directors has chosen to rescue Chrysler are described by the press in almost mystical and heroic terms. Such is especially the case with the president of Chrysler, Lee Iacocca.

One of the most important results of Broms and Gahmberg's analysis is that they are able to demonstrate that many of the different roles in the Proppian and Greimasian scheme are played by the same actor. Thus, for instance, the real subject of both the Chrysler drama and the sender (the initiator of the story) is actually the Great American Economy, with all its glaring strengths and weaknesses. Consider, too, the nature of the adversaries. It is not clear that the adversaries are merely Chrysler's competitors (Ford, GM, the Japanese) or whether a good part of the problem is actually Chrysler itself, with its outmoded management, its failure to read correctly the market's signals, and so forth. At a deeper level, the greatest fear is that the "real enemy" is truly unknown—nameless fear itself—

and that nobody knows what is really in store. That is, the real enemy is everything and nothing. As Broms and Gahmberg note, "Chrysler is suffering [as *Business Week* put it], from an 'Orphan Syndrome'—everybody is leaving the sinking ship. There seems to be a sense of fear about something unknowable coming. There is the fear of the whole auto industry being orphanized; one illustrative subtitle is 'Detroit's Fate' " (1980, p. 16).

Broms and Gahmberg make an exceedingly important observation when they note that in this drama Chrysler is both the party that is helped and the helper at the same time:

> The helper is a metaphysical principle that helps the world of the spectacle to go on. In the Chrysler crisis spectacle we may see the American economic system as a cosmic value, as a central theme. As the auto industry and Chrysler [are] . . . important elements in this very system [that is, economic], we have . . . the situation . . . where Chrysler is both the helped and the helper [at the same time]. However, in the Greimasian spectacle Chrysler also seems to be a receiver, for example, a larger entity, a system, which is the beneficiary of the Cosmic Order (which is the same as the American economic system). In the press Chrysler's leaders are accused of snatching too much of that Cosmic order. The counter remark of one Chrysler Vice President about the federal aid program illustrates this: "It's all or nothing" [*Business World,* December 1979, cited in Broms and Gahmberg, 1980, pp. 16-17].

Perhaps the most telling and literal illustration of the fact that Chrysler is perceived as simultaneously fulfilling a number of different roles in this drama was revealed in a cartoon in *Business Week* (December 24,1979). A dwarf-sized Uncle Sam is trying to fill a huge flat tire symbolizing Chrysler itself.

The chilling question that Broms and Gahmberg raise at the end of their analysis, and one that I believe is precisely *the* right one, is: Is the Chrysler episode a modern example dressed up in metal of the archetypal American story, *Moby Dick*? "The study of the actant [that is, stakeholder or role character] utterances about the issue gives reason to say that the leaders of the auto industry, in this case particularly Lee Iacocca, are seen as Captain Ahabs, who are called to lead the Cosmic Van toward a sacred goal. At the time of this analysis the self-evidence of the goal is being shattered, [hence] the prevailing concern about the unknowable to come in the views of the actants [stakeholders] " (Broms and Gahmberg, 1980, p. 19).

I have dwelt on the Proppian and Greimasian scheme of analysis and the use to which Broms and Gahmberg have put it for a number of reasons. First, perhaps the most distinguishing characteristic that separates scientific from nonscientific stories is that nonscientific stories, as I have constantly stressed, are intensely personalized. That is, in nonscientific stories the functions are explicitly carried by intensely human stakeholders, whereas in scientific stories they tend to remain as pure, depersonalized, abstract entities or classes (for example, Evidence, Warrant, Claim, and so on). Two, in scientific stories the attempt is made (not always successfully) to keep the separate aspects strictly at bay in separate categories. Indeed, one is generally admonished not to mix categories, not to make category mistakes, as they are called.

The force, however, of a nonscientific story often derives in large part from the fact that one character may take on or play different roles simultaneously. The reason is not only that the structure of characters, stories, and situations are extremely complicated in life (complication is an integral part of life) but that complication adds to the essential plausibility or believability of a character. There is no such thing as an uncomplicated, pure, or uncontaminated character in reality.

For all their differences from scientific stories, the stories of this section are better named as "in-between" or ego stories. This is because neither Propp, Greimas, Broms, nor Gahmberg seems to penetrate to the level of archetypes. Even though there is a strong recognition of the mythological element that penetrates and permeates all stories, no matter how realistic they attempt to be, the focus of their analyses is still primarily on real characters, that is, on the ego level of reality. In the case of the Chrysler story for instance, it is relatively easy to get the major drift, point, or moral of the story. This mode does not penetrate to the level of analysis of stories from an archetypal perspective. For this reason, archetypal stories are treated separately in the next section.

The point is that "in-between" stories are truly in-between. They share a number of common features with both scientific and archetypal stories—the complete opposite ends of the spectrum. With scientific stories, they share a rather fixed and limited structure. Propp's basic observations regarding fairy tales reveal this limiting structure: "(1) *[The] functions of [the] characters [in fairy tales] serve as stable, constant elements in a tale, independent of how and by whom they are fulfilled;* (2) *The number of functions known to the fairy tale is limited* (Propp, 1968, p. 21); (3) *The sequence of functions is always identical* (p. 22); (4) *All fairy tales are of one type in regard to their structure"* (p. 23).

None of these apply, or only in a very restrictive and limited sense, to archetypal stories. In-between or ego-state stories, however, share with archetypal stories an emphasis on metaphors and mythological themes. However, it is precisely the *acknowledged* range and depth of fictitious elements that separates archetypal from all other kinds of stories.

Archetypal Stories

Step by step, we have been steadily approaching the conclusion that archetypal stories, that is, the stories through which archetypes reveal and display themselves, are very different both in principle and in structure from scientific and egoic stories. I know of no one who has caught better the essence of the difference between scientific, egoic, and archetypal stories than the eminent Jungian analyst James Hillman (1975b). For this reason, we will attempt to follow Hillman in his insightful, penetrating analysis of the matter.

Essentially, I believe, there are three major points to Hillman's analysis. The first concerns the basically and deliberately fictional character of the case histories that are presented and recorded in psychotherapeutic/psychoanalytic sessions. The second concerns the basic differences in plots between the kinds of fictions that are recorded/written by Freudian and Jungian ana-

lysts. The third concerns the fact that the main character (the
patient) in his or her fiction/story/dream is a profoundly divided and split person. The main character (the patient), in
short, is a player who plays and adopts many roles within the
structure of a fictional story of his or her creation. Each of the
parts of the story is, as it were, contained almost entirely within the psyche of the subject.

Regarding the first point, early on in his investigations,
Freud discovered that the case histories of his patients were not
histories that were literally true. Rather, they were purposeful,
deliberate reconstructions. They were invented fantasies designed to hide from both the analyst and the patients themselves what "really happened." Their purpose was to help the patient construct an "as-if" world that fitted in with the kind of
accommodation the patient was able to strike between his or
her character structure and the surrounding environment.

If the patient constructs a fiction—indeed, has to construct one—then his or her problem *is* the fiction that has been
constructed. If this is so, then according to Hillman (1975b),
the problem that therapy seeks to resolve is the "successful"
reconstitution of the patient's story (internal and external history, self-image, self-perception, and so on). I quote:

> Successful therapy is thus a collaboration between fic-
> tions, a revisioning of the [individual patient's or, in the case
> where the entire family system is at fault, the family's] story
> into a more intelligent, more imaginative plot, which also means
> the sense of mythos in all parts of the story.
> Unfortunately, we therapists are not aware enough that
> we are "singers" [that is, arrangers between different kinds of
> fictions]. We miss a lot of what we could be doing. Our ways of
> narration are limited to four kinds: epic, comic, detective, social
> realism. We take what comes—no matter how passionate and
> erotic, how tragic and noble, how freakish and arbitrary—and
> turn it all into one of our four modes. First, there are the cases
> showing the ego's development, especially out of childhood,
> through obstacles and defeats: heroic epic [see Chapter Six].
> Second, the tales of the tangles, the confused identities and un-
> certain genders, the impossible bumbling inadequacies of the
> foolish victim, but which come out with a happy end of adjust-

ment: comic. Third, unmasking hidden plots through clues and crises, indefatigably tracking down what went wrong by a taciturn but twinkle-eyed, pipe-puffing analyst, not too unlike Holmes or Poirot: detective. Fourth, the detailed descriptions of small circumstances, true to life, the family as a misfortune, environmental conditions as another, historicism as verbatim accounts of the actual milieu, all presented with lugubrious sociological terminology and the heavy-handed panned shots of tendentious importance: social realism [Hillman, 1975b, p. 140].

The second point concerns the profound differences between Freudian and Jungian plots or plotting. From the perspective that we have been exploring, that is, case-histories as fiction, the greatest charge of criticism that a Jungian can level against a Freudian is that Freud's plots are too simple. They are all of the same basic kind. This same criticism also applies to the method of storytelling of the previous two sections. Conversely, a Freudian could legitimately charge a Jungian with unduly complicating the story. As Hillman, as a Jungian and thereby as a partisan observer, puts it: "Basic plot in Freud is simple. Every Freudian narrative comes out the same way and can be taken apart to show one answer to the question *why*. The mystery is repression (in one of many varieties), followed by passions, crimes, miseries (symptom formation), the involvement of the author (transference of the repressed), lifting of the repression through prolonged recognition (psychotherapy), and the denouement of ending therapy. When Jung charges Freud with too simplistic a causal schema, he is faulting Freud for his plotting" (1975b, pp. 130-131).

In short, Jung's plotting is considerably more complicated. His theory of plotting echoes his theory of archetypes. Each archetype, while it may be contained in all other archetypes (see Chapter Six), has nonetheless its own distinct story to tell (von Franz, 1981). Each archetype has its distinct tale and place in the stories of an individual's psyche and in an institution's history.

As a result, Jung's form of plotting is "inherently multiplistic and variegated" (Hillman, 1975b, p. 131). The paths by which individuals reach individuation or resolution are so varied, so unique, that no one individual plot (archetype) is sufficient to capture the essence of an individual's story. As a result, there is a certain fundamental ineffability in the understanding of human behavior. Whether that means that there cannot therefore be a science of human behavior at the deepest levels is another matter. I believe that there can be such a science but that it is very different in form from science traditionally conceived. The discussion of such a matter is the topic of Chapter Nine.

Hillman hits home most precisely when he notes that *the* basic difference between Freud and Jung is the difference between allegory and metaphor. The equation is: Freud is to allegory, particularly its reductive explanation (for example, the myth of Oedipus), as Jung is to metaphor, especially its nonreductive explanation. The difference between the two is profound and essential: "both start off saying one thing as if it were another" (Hillman, 1975b, p. 157). In this sense, both seem to be the same. But it is precisely at this point that they diverge sharply. Allegory divides its subject matter into two distinct entities whereas metaphor does not. Allegory divides the subject matter of its story into a manifest or surface part and a latent or beneath the surface (that is, less visibly interpreted or seen) part. Furthermore, allegory then interpretatively translates the manifest or surface symbol into the latent or beneath the surface symbol. The metaphorical method, however, "keeps the two voices together, hearing the dream as it tells itself, ambiguously evocative and concretely precise at each and every instant. Metaphors are not subject to interpretative translation without breaking up their peculiar unity" (Hillman, 1975b, p. 157) (see, especially, Lakoff and Johnson, 1980, on this point).

Finally, a primary feature of archetypal stories or of stories where archetypes are featured prominently is that the person who is the subject of the story tends to play all the roles simultaneously. Unlike scientific and egoic stories where the parts are clearly labeled, identified, and kept neatly apart, this does not happen in archetypal stories. The fact that the subject plays all parts is meant to stand for the compartmentalized nature of the psyche. (For one of the best treatments of this see von Franz, 1980.) It is meant to reflect the basic dismemberment that is characteristic of the human psyche as it has developed and evolved in human culture to date (Wilber, 1981b):

> The actor is and is not, a person and a persona [mask], divided and undivided—as Dionysus. The self divided is precisely where the self is authentically located—contrary to Laing. Authenticity is in the perpetual dismemberment of being and not-being a self, a being that is always in many parts, like a dream with a full cast. We all have identity crises because a single identity is a delusion of the monotheistic mind that would defeat Dionysus at all costs. We all have dispersed consciousness through all our body parts, wandering wombs; we are all hysterics. Authenticity is *in* the illusion, playing it, seeing through it from within as we play it, like an actor who sees through his mask and can only see it this way [Hillman, 1975b, pp. 160–161].

Recently, Joanne Martin and her students (1982) at Stanford have been studying actual stories in real organizations. They discovered, for instance, that all organizations seem to have a character in their history who fits the Horatio Alger story. Similarly, all organizations seem to have some version of a "bringing-the-leader-down-to-size," an equalizing or humanizing the leader, type story. The difference between egoic and archetypal stories is precisely this. In egoic stories some other character external to the central character brings him or her down to size. In archetypal stories, an aspect of the character's own psyche (that is, an archetypal force) does battle with and brings the character's psyche down to size. Again, von Franz (1980) is an excellent source on this.

In conclusion, the question we have come to is: Can the stakeholders that constitute the mind and society, which are now so variegated and so separated from one another that they can be said to suffer severe disassociation, be reunited? This is the subject of Chapters Nine and Ten.

CHAPTER NINE

New Perspectives on Organizations and Social Science

Every rule of behavior which you can deduce from the unconscious is usually a paradox [von Franz, 1980, p. 257].

In this chapter we confront once again some of the most basic questions that plague any treatment of stakeholders and archetypes. These issues are set in motion by the very nature of our subject matter. They have continually built as we have proceeded through this volume. Among them are What forces are responsible for setting in motion the existence of archetypes and stakeholders?; why are they so disparate and so fragmented?; what are the prospects for a greater reunification between archetypes and stakeholders?; and what is a proper method or scope of inquiry for knowing archetypes and stakeholders?

All of these questions are inherently philosophical. They cannot even be approached independently of a philosophical conception as to how the various known sciences fit together. If there was ever anything that demanded an interdisciplinary or a transdisciplinary theory of inquiry, it is clearly the study of archetypes and stakeholders. Archetypes and stakeholders cut across every conceivable branch of knowledge. Neither their nature nor their properties can be captured or exhausted by any

139

single branch of knowledge. Thus, it behooves us to discuss what a truly interdisciplinary theory of inquiry (Churchman, 1971, 1979) looks like, not merely to say that one is necessary.

A deeper reason for discussing philosophical concerns is that a response to the questions raised earlier involves an archetype, that is, an archetypal conception of the relationship between the various branches of science. As a result, we need to discuss several archetypal conceptions of science so that we can finally address the questions that are our primary concern. A by-product of this discussion is the outline of a different agenda for the human sciences and the prospects for a different methodology for studying its special subject matter. Above all, it promises to shed light on the most important and fundamental question of all: Toward what does the psyche of humanity and thereby its institutions seem to be evolving? We begin by discussing two radically different conceptions of the structure of science.

Two Archetypal Conceptions of Science

Two archetypal patterns emerge repeatedly in exploring the relationship between the sciences. One is that of a strict hierarchical pattern. The other is that of a complete lack of hierarchy. Whereas in the first pattern some, typically one or a very select few, sciences are regarded as more basic or fundamental than all others, in the second, all sciences are regarded as on an equal footing. Whereas the first is naturally or inherently reductionistic, the second is inherently systemic.

Nowhere are these two archetypal patterns presented and contrasted more vividly than in the works of the philosophers of social science, C. West Churchman (1961, 1971) and his mentor E. A. Singer (1959). Churchman and Singer present the strongest possible form of the hierarchical archetype, but they are not advocates of it. Their purpose is rather to examine it, to show what follows from it, and ultimately to show how their own philosophy of science, or more broadly speaking, philosophy of inquiry, is founded on the opposite archetype. Their examination is thus in the form of a gigantic "what if"—what if the sciences were organized in a linear hierarchical fashion?

Churchman and Singer begin their examination by asking, "What if the sciences were arrayed from the supposedly 'most basic' or 'fundamental' down to the less basic or less fundamental; what science or sciences would head the list; and what would the relation between the sciences be?" The work of the positivists supplies a response to all three questions (Popper, 1972).*

From time immemorial, logic and mathematics have been proposed as perennial candidates for the most basic or fundamental of the sciences. Why? Because every science in its basic desire to reason clearly presupposes the prior existence of the science of logic. For instance, all of the sciences place an exceedingly high premium on the concept of logical consistency. Quite simply, it is taken for granted, if it is not regarded as a basic law of reasoning, that an assertion or a proposition cannot be both true and false at the same time. Thus, logic, even before that of mathematics, is the leading candidate for the status of the most basic science. Furthermore, the relationship between the sciences is established by means of the concept *presupposes*. Thus, one science X is more basic than another science Y if Y presupposes the theoretical concepts or notions of science X but X does not presuppose the concepts or notions of Y.

Having introduced the supposedly most basic science, logic, and the relationship between the sciences the concept presupposes, Churchman and Singer gave an illustration of what the ordered list of sciences looks like. The word *illustration* is important, for my purpose here is not to give an exact placement or classification of every known science but rather to sketch the general nature of the hierarchy. Also, it should be understood that the concept of a science being treated in this discussion is very broad. It is well known, for instance, by contemporary sociologists of science, that there is as much variance within a scientific discipline as there is between them (Chubin, 1976). Increasingly, the unit of sociological analysis within sci-

---

*Note that, from my perspective, Popper is to be regarded as a positivist, for he strongly affirms the separation between sciences. Indeed, he has so little regard for the social sciences that he treats them with contempt.

ence is that of the subdiscipline or subspeciality. For our purposes, however, I shall ignore these fine points, for my thesis is not dependent upon them.

I also shall not bother to pursue in fine detail the complete listing of the sciences arrayed just below logic. What is more important to note is that the hierarchy or taxonomy of the sciences is split in half. At the top half is arrayed the mathematical and the physical sciences, with logic serving as the "queen" of the sciences. At the bottom half is arrayed the social sciences. This reflects the all-too-common, taken-for-granted presumption of the superiority of the physical sciences over the social. That is, on every conceivable dimension the physical sciences are supposed to be superior to the social. Supposedly they are more exact, more precise, more theoretically sound, better grounded, "harder," and so on.

Lurking within the hierarchy are two other important ideas. Every science introduces special terms, concepts, and ideas that are distinctively its own. Thus, for instance, logic introduces the concepts of logical laws, logical operators, elementary propositions, sentences, valid forms of reasoning, incorrect forms of reasoning, and so forth. (See, for example, the discussion of valid reasoning in science in Chapter Eight.) Physics, for another, introduces such concepts as energy, force, mass, spatial coordinate systems, conservation laws of energy, in general, the basic idea of the universe as a physical entity.

A critical issue in all such orderings concerns whether the concepts of a science Y farther down in the list can be strictly derived from or assimilated in terms of the concepts of a science X higher up in the list of the sciences. If all the concepts of Y can be shown to follow from those of X, then science Y can be said to be "reducible to" that of X. This is, in brief, the thesis of reductionism. Notice that the concept of presupposes is looser or broader than that of reductionism. Under the concept of presupposition, we need merely show that *some* of the more important aspects of science Y *depend* upon those of science X. Reductionism is thus the strongest form of arraying the list of the various sciences.

A critical juncture is reached when we encounter the science of biology. All living things as members of the physical world must, as a result, be subject to physical and chemical processes. They must thereby obey physical and chemical laws. It is precisely because this idea exerts such a hold on the human imagination that a very strong difficulty is encountered. We are not presently able to reduce all of humanity's complex mental and social phenomena to, say, neurophysiological models, laws, or phenomena, although there is no question that our capability for doing this has grown enormously (Jaynes, 1976). The difficulty concerns the fact that all purported explanations of living things *solely* in physical terms run into a fundamental difficulty. For every suggested formal rule or physical law that purports to explain or to separate clearly the living from the nonliving, one has always been able to find certain nonliving things that somehow pass the rule and ought therefore to count as a living thing, and certain living things that somehow fail the rule and ought therefore to fall into the category of the nonliving. It is not that there are not differences between the two classes. There obviously are differences. It is rather that some of the differences are impossible to capture in *fixed, formalized, logical or physical laws/rules*. Thus, for example, certain insects neither reproduce themselves nor display metabolic processes but certain machines can "reproduce" themselves and certain chemicals and even modern buildings display "metabolic" processes.

The upshot of the discussion is that modern philosophers of biology have been forced back time and again to the concept of teleology or purposefulness in order to separate the living from the nonliving. In this sense the concept of living things is not *solely* or *strictly* reducible to physical laws or processes.

It should be noted that by teleology or purposefulness I do not mean a mysterious "elan vital" that inhabits all living creatures but rather the systematic scientific study of those purposes that a *person*, the biological scientist, *imputes* to those organisms he or she studies (Churchman, 1961, 1971). Indeed, the very sciences whose function it is to study why the biological scientist imputes particular kinds of purposes to other organisms, are none other than the psychology and sociology of science. These sciences have as *their* special purview other scientists and why scientists reason as they do, both individually and collectively as part of an organized social community. To continue the story, however, biology has brought us to the second or lower half of the taxonomy, the social sciences.

For initial purposes, it suffices to say that the social sciences are distinguished by the "size" of the social organism they treat. Thus, if biology treats the smallest and lowest orders of living things, then psychology is the so-called first of the social sciences to treat higher order living things. In particular, the newer humanistic and depth psychologies have taken it as their special purview to treat the whole human being, and not merely one or more of his or her special parts, aspects, or drives.

If psychology, generally speaking, treats the autonomous, self-contained, whole human being, then the subject matter of sociology, generally speaking, ranges from that of the small group to that of a whole human society. Once again it is here that reductionism raises its troublesome head. *If* a group is nothing more than the sum of its separate parts, *then* the science of sociology in general, and at the very least the subject matter of small group behavior in particular, ought in principle to be reducible to psychology or to psychological phenomena. The critical term in the preceding sentence is, of course, the word *if*. The critical question is whether *all* of group behavior is reducible to individual behavior or whether there are some properties that groups have which none of their individual members possess. Chapter Seven has argued, in effect, that the answer to the latter question is "yes" even though the line is exceedingly thin between individuals and groups. Groups can develop a more heightened experience of certain archetypes than the individuals that compose the group, and vice versa.

Because of its perpetual philosophical and practical importance, the issue will undoubtedly continue to be debated as long as there are philosophers and social scientists. Suffice it to say that there are exceedingly powerful arguments and sets of evidence on both sides of the controversy. Indeed, it seems that this will always be the case. The evidence and arguments will always be mixed because, if only in part, we are dealing with an issue that is as much metaphysical as it is scientific. Issues such as the reducibility of one science to that of another are not of the character of factual judgments that can be answered by a simple "yes" or "no." They are what I have called ill-structured problems in contrast to well-structured exercises.

Paradoxically, precisely because the evidence is mixed, and it seems that it will always be, there is good reason to regard sociology as a distinct, if not separate, science. That is, it treats phenomena not all of which can be reduced to psychological explanation. Sociology's distinctness, however, does not mean that the subject matter of psychology, sociology, economics, or political science, to mention only a few, does not overlap considerably. It also does not mean that because sociology treats a larger social collectivity that it is necessarily any less basic a science than psychology. It is only less basic in the linear, hierarchical archetype I have been exploring.

If sociology takes as a unit of analysis the concept of the group and of society, then anthropology takes the concept of culture as its fundamental precept and focuses on the systematic differences between societies. History, however, treats the largest of all human groups—humanity—and seeks to discover whatever generalized patterns of actions and purposes characterize human societies viewed in the broadest possible sense. With considerable reluctance history has only recently been admitted as a social science. Hence, it is understandable why the reluctance to consider theology as a social science is even more severe. Leaving this debate aside, we can recognize nonetheless that theology treats the largest human *experience* imaginable—contemplation of the nature of the entire universe.

This in very brief completes the linear, hierarchical archetype of the ordering of the sciences. It is linear because it views the sciences as preceding strictly from the most theoretically certain and sound, the most rigorous, down to the least theoretically certain, the most contentious, and the least rigorous. There is, however, another view of the relationship between the sciences that opposes the linear archetype in nearly every respect. This opposite archetype can be called a circle or a wheel to distinguish it from the linear. The wheel archetype is less

commonly held or expressed because it is based on a less widely
adhered to style of inquiry (Mitroff and Kilmann, 1978). It goes
largely against the grain of traditional scientific thinking and the
premises that underlie the current organization of the university.

In a word, the circular archetype is founded on the radical notion that *all of the sciences presuppose one another in the
sense that the concepts of all the sciences have a bearing on one
another* (Churchman, 1971). As such, there are no fundamental
or more basic sciences. Some sciences may be more developed
along some lines or criteria than others, but there is no science
that is equally developed along all lines or criteria. Thus, if one
science is more basic or more fundamental according to some
criteria, then it is less basic or less fundamental according to
some other criteria. Instead of a posture of intellectual superiority or arrogance, the wheel archetype regards the relationship
between the sciences as one of mutual complementation and
support, not opposition or competition.

Consider physics and sociology. There is no doubt that
historically sociology owes a tremendous debt to physics. Physics has continually supplied sociology with a powerful set of
organizing concepts and metaphors. For example, some of the
earliest attempts at building explanatory models of society were
clearly governed by Newtonian metaphors. Thus, by analogy,
society was conceived as a mass acted on by a series of propelling
and restraining forces. The net sum of these forces causes society to move in certain directions with a certain acceleration,
and so forth.

What is not so clear and far more contentious is that sociology has anything to offer to seemingly so exalted a science
as physics. Some, such as Popper, deny this vehemently. Yet it
is precisely this very proposition that the wheel archetype asserts. What the wheel archetype contends is that the science of
physics has presupposed without its conscious awareness a very
complex social organization (Swatez, 1966). Indeed, it is precisely because physics has taken its social side so much for
granted that it has failed to acknowledge its debt to such social
sciences as sociology.

To be more specific, one must consider the fact that all

of science is the product of a complex set of social and institutional forces that have brought it into being and have sustained its existence. For all practical purposes (very practical, indeed), physics today is Big Physics, that is, the leading member of Big Science (Price, 1963). We are indeed far from the day of the great physicist Maxwell fooling around with magnets in his garage. The physicist of today instead plays with very big and expensive machines called cyclotrons and bevatrons. These machines, which are used to penetrate the structure of the atom, are very costly to build and to operate. They demand, as a result, a complex social and institutional structure both to design and to operate them. For instance, not everyone who so desires it can gain access to these machines and hence perform his or her favored experiment.

Now one could contend that the criteria used to allocate precious time on these machines, a valuable and costly resource, are purely objective and flow perfectly from the principles of physics so that physics has no need of sociology and management theory. Note carefully the word *contend*. Unfortunately, the growing evidence—be it noted *scientific*—from the psychology and sociology of science does not support these contentions (Mitroff, 1974). To the contrary, the evidence is that a wide variety of criteria enter into the selection of those who are allowed to run their experiments and that many of these criteria are social in nature, for instance, the experimenter's "perceived" psychological and professional standing in the physics community, the "prestige" of the university where one is currently located, where one received one's first degree, and so on. This is not to say that this situation is necessarily wrong. Such criteria are to be expected to operate in all complex social systems. Our physical science would have to be far more developed than it is currently or will ever be to expect a set of purely impersonal, objective rules to be able to select the best experiment out of all those proposed. If there is thus anything wrong, it is instead the lack of acknowledgment of the tremendous role that social processes play in physical science.

To take another example, consider the fact that nuclear science often demands the scanning of literally thousands of photographs to detect the occurrence of a significant but rare nuclear event. Now, whether or not the scanning is completely automated, and to this date it has not been possible to automate the entire process, principles have to be specified for the detection of critical events by a *human observer*. Thus, a psychological entity is presupposed. As studies of radar operators during the Second World War revealed, it is no easy task to motivate operators to maintain a high level of awareness and vigilance to notice rare events out of thousands of background events—a finding reminiscent of the astronomer Bessel's difficulties in finding reliable observers. The upshot is that the design of an effective monitoring system is not entirely a physical science problem. If one pursues the issue entirely in physical terms, one neglects important knowledge and variables to be gained from another science. It is akin to seeking a quantum mechanical explanation of love when a psychological or a literary explanation is what one should seek.

Finally, consider one last example, the relation between logic and history. It is clear that in its desire to produce clear, consistent explanations of phenomena, history presupposes logic. But is there any sense in which logic presupposes history? There is, if we consider the fact that what Western civilization considers to be the immutable laws of logical thought are not universally shared by all cultures. Thus history must offer logic different presuppositions, concepts, or notions upon which to build a science of logic or of reasoning. As Churchman (1971) has so cogently put it, logic in the broader sense ought to be considered as a branch of communication theory or social psychology, not solely as a branch of abstract mathematics or reasoning.

The point of the discussion is that we are dealing with two very different conceptions, psychologies, if you will, of the organization of knowledge. One cannot strictly prove, as it were, that one archetype is right and the other is wrong. Fundamentally this is not of the nature of archetypes (Jung, 1923). The nature of what constitutes an adequate proof of an archetype is not something that stands apart from an archetype itself. This is one of the basic points of archetypal stories discussed in Chapter Eight. The guarantor of the validity of an archetype is all wrapped up, as it were, as part of the story context in which archetypes exert a hold on the human mind.

This does not mean that one cannot compare archetypes and note their consequences, for this is precisely what I have done. All it means is that in the end we have to realize that the way people chose to conceive of the relationships among the various branches of knowledge is itself a massive projective test. However, it also means that when a scientist argues that one discipline is *inherently* better or superior in all its respects to that of another, he or she is no longer being purely scientific. Instead, we are learning about that scientist's psychological preferences (Mitroff, 1974; Mitroff and Kilmann, 1978). Note very carefully that I am *not* saying that the judgment of acceptable or outstanding work within a discipline can be reduced solely to psychology or sociology. That would be reverse reductionism on a grand scale. Rather, the contention is that *elements* of psychology and sociology infect and influence but do not determine every aspect of humanity's work.

If some of the most critical parts of policy arguments (see Chapters Two, Three, and Eight) are propositions of the kind stakeholder X affects or have a property that affects stakeholder Y, then practically speaking, it makes a great difference regarding which archetype one adopts. If the variables that characterize stakeholder properties are a mixture of behavioral and physical considerations and if they are to be given equal weight and serious consideration, then I believe that the adoption of the wheel archetype is fundamental to the applied social sciences.

From the standpoint of the applied social sciences, the linear archetype is more than just inappropriate; it is silly, an outworn image of an earlier age. However, for this reason, there will probably always be a fundamental tension between the so-called pure and applied sciences. The pure (that is, disciplinary) sciences generally adhere to the linear archetype with the attendant consequence that those sciences that are judged to be farther down in the list suffer from an inferiority complex. To use Toffler's (1980) terminology, such an inferiority complex may indeed have been justified during the "second-wave," when the industrial revolution was in bloom and when science, particularly physical science, became of age. However, during the "third-wave," the electronic age, where everything affects everything else, this attitude is no longer something we can afford. In a word, we can no longer afford the separation of the various sciences nor the reliance on an outmoded philosophy of positivism and reductionism.

John Carroll (1978) has constructed a fascinating typology of seven different types of intellectuals. In terms of Carroll's typology, it can be seen that the underlying image we have of the university is due primarily to two types, the Mandarin (the power-seeking disciplinarian) and the Chess Player (the abstract mathematician). These are the types whose image of knowledge, the linear archetype, is the one that prevails. The Mandarin and the Chess Player are so locked into their image of knowledge and take it so much for granted, that they are unable to even acknowledge other archetypal conceptions. By itself, this is reason enough to account for the extremity of the reactions that the highly unorthodox philosopher of science Paul Feyerabend (1978) and his opponents set off in one another.

Feyerabend is a type of person who is rarely seen in philosophy of science quarters. Where the overwhelming majority of contemporary philosophers of science are of the Mandarin and Chess Player variety, Feyerabend is a unique blend of the Chiliast (the dreamer: he has highly orthodox *visions* of an alternate conception of science), the Shaman (the healer: he wants science to be a force for healing society), the Galahad (the wandering scholar: his quest is the use of science for betterment), and the King's Fool (he loves to taunt his adversaries and to rub their ignorance in their faces). Feyerabend not only chastises his fellow philosophers for their disciplinary narrowness but also, in his words, for their "professional incompetence":

Given nothing but the criteria of the average philosopher of science . . . it is . . . impossible to recognize irony, metaphor, playful exaggeration. Yet writers who have studied these categories, who have examined them in the work of others and who use them in their own creations, are not at all at a loss, they make their judgments with minimal error and with perfect ease. True, their "criteria" do not occur in the standard works on philosophy of science. But they can be learned, applied, refined. It is simply not true that a writer who leaves the domain of rational [i.e., Mandarin and Chess Player] discourse ceases to make sense and that a reader who follows him is left without a guide, though it must appear so to those who have only read Popper and Carnap and never even heard of Lessing, Mencken, Tucholsky [1978, p. 184].

All of the distinctions of [the Mandarin, disciplinary philosophy of science] (context of discovery/context of justification; logical/psychological; internal/external; and so on) have but one aim: to turn incompetence (ignorance of relevant material and lack of imagination) into expertise (happy assurance that the things not known and unimaginable are not relevant and that it would be professionally incompetent to use them) [1978, p. 202].

Whither Archetypes and the Fragmentation of Western Peoples

Nowhere is the link between the nature of archetypes, the images that humanity produces of the future, and the archetypal images we have of the various branches of knowledge made stronger than in the work of Ken Wilber (1981b). Wilber's work stands out above all others in this area. Drawing upon nearly every one of the eleven social scientists whom we designated in the preface as being our leading guides, Wilber has fashioned the most complete, comprehensive, and integrative theory of archetypes and their relation to social evolution to date. There is no way that one can do adequate justice to a book as rich as his in a brief summary. Therefore, without any pretensions of justice whatsoever, let me try to capture the essence of his all-too-important message.

Like Neumann (1970) and the other social scientists referred to in the preface, Wilber postulates that the historical evolution of the development of a person's psyche can be deciphered if one knows how to read the appropriate records. The appropriate records in this case are those that are revealed by the wide mixture of disciplines associated with the eleven guides singled out for special mention in the preface, that is, anthropology, depth psychology, mythology, comparative religion, and so on. The appropriate reading of the appropriate records in this case is a highly complex blending of anthropological, archetypal, historical, and philosophical interpretation.

Wilber's (1981b) theory of the evolution of the psyche holds that through the historical writings we have available we are able to glimpse the major psychological problems that the persons of a given era were struggling with by means of the major archetypes dominant in the writings of that period. Thus, in the very beginning of all beginnings, the Bible portrays man and woman in a literal, uroboric fusion with nature; they are truly asleep and in this sense know no sin for they "know" nothing; they are not yet capable of anything except instinctive animal-like knowing at this stage. In this sense, Wilber rightly rebukes the idea of returning to the Garden of Eden as an end to our current woes as a romanticist folly. It is a return to a presleep. As Jaynes (1976) and Wilber argue, in the beginning a human being's waking and dreamlike states were almost totally fused together. Humans lived in a dream and heard dreamlike voices penetrating their everyday "waking life," if it can be called that. True, there are no problems in this state but neither is there awareness. There is nothing that we know as conscious mind. The solution of the return to the Garden of Eden is thus truly as severe as the problems.

The stage of evolution characterized by the recognition that one has a physical body is governed by typhonic archetypes. These are the archetypes we encountered in Chapter Six. They are bizarre mixtures of half-human and half-animal. As we saw, these designate that the psyche of humans is not completely differentiated from their animal or instinctual nature—they have not yet fully separated themselves from the animal kingdom. Hence, they still identify to a considerable degree with animals and both perceive and describe themselves in terms of animal properties.

Wilber traces in a brilliant, painstaking, and scholarly way the traces and the steps in the evolution of mind. He argues convincingly that each stage of the development of a person's psyche demanded the severest wrenching from the hold that the archetype of the preceding stage exercised. He also argues that "each *stage* of development embodies a *mode* of self, and further, what is the *whole* of the self at one stage forms merely a *part* of the whole of the next. But not all of the old self is *consciously* [emphasis added] carried by the new self. Once a stage is superseded by its successor, that *stage* itself becomes a *level* of the individual, or a *conscious component* of the higher self. However, the old *mode* of self does *not* become a conscious component of the next mode of self, but is relegated to the submergent unconscious" (Wilber, 1981b, p. 53).

Wilber argues that, at present, we have achieved stage 4, or the intermediate level of development, in his eightfold theory. To get from stage 3 to stage 4 demanded that people wrestle themselves free from one of the strongest, most terrifying and devouring of all the archetypes that humanity has been able to fathom to date—the Great Mother. As explained in Chapters Six and Seven, unless an individual successfully fights the battle of slaying the Dragon Mother, he or she will not only remain in an undeveloped state but will be swallowed up by the Mother's psyche, that is, fall back into unconsciousness (much as the hero of the current movie *TRON* falls into the computer). However, Wilber and a host of other major social thinkers contend that the feat of obtaining sustained emancipation from the hold of the earliest Great Mother cults, myths, and societies was so psychologically demanding, especially in Western European peoples, that the early fragile psyche overemancipated itself to the point of fragmentation. Thus, perhaps the most basic response to the question of why the existence of stakeholders and their extreme specialization or fragmentation in Western peoples is "because of the incredible energy demands placed upon an immature, developing ego—not only to achieve separation from the hold of the Mother in the first place but to sustain it with any degree of permanency in the second place." I quote from Wilber: "Although at [the] early typhonic stage the mind and body are predifferentiated, the typhon itself is beginning to separate from the environment. . . . It is therefore faced with primitive forms of dread, anxiety, and the terror [that is, first realization] of death. . . . In order to survive . . . with a minimum of terror, the self has to begin to close its eyes; to numb itself; to tighten down its own activities and sequester its own vitality. *To avoid death, it has to dilute [that is, fragment] life"* (1981b, p. 211).

For many of the same reasons, I believe that this is why people are afraid to join an organization. They are afraid that an essential part of their uniqueness will be swallowed up by the mass. When this happens, a critical part of one's essential self, that is, what Jungians call the Self or the deepest innermost layer of the psyche, is threatened with loss. What occurs as a result of this fear is one of the most fascinating negotiations between the organization and the individual. In return for collective power and action, the individual gives certain critical parts of his or her psyche to the organization. But if this is so, then it also helps to explain why each organization has a unique cast. The unique side of each organization is composed of the sum (that is, interaction) of the archetypes that each individual contributes or gives up in order to join the mass. This in itself helps to identify one of the most neglected aspects of organization behavior: the study of the uniqueness of all organizations.

It will not go unnoticed that Wilber places the present environment of humanity squarely in the middle of the ultimate possibilities he envisages. Now, *the* 64 billion dollar question for Wilber and everyone else is, "How do we *know* that there are these other possibilities of further development, and that there are roughly eight in all?" Wilber gives the only answer that is possible for a question of this type. The eight stages emerge from a prolonged and protracted study of the "higher stages of consciousness" that the very exalted few and hence *the* supreme archetypal role models of human civilization have been able to achieve. Among these are the Buddha and Christ.

Wilber contends that there are, roughly speaking, only two distinct ways of achieving reunification of the extreme—the disassociation of archetypes, and hence of the psyche—that characterizes modern humanity. The first is to fall back into the original "fall," the original garden of unconsciousness. This he rightly dismisses as romantic nonsense. The second is through the path of transcendence, that is, super- or transconsciousness as represented by *the* archetypes of higher consciousness, that is, Buddha or Christ.

By now it is readily apparent that we are frankly in the realm of the religious, the Spiritual. More than that we are squarely in the realm of archetypal knowledge. This is why so much time was spent earlier in this chapter discussing in general the significance of the two great archetypes of inquiry—the line and the wheel. If anything, Wilber's concept of evolution is a combination of the two since it is by his own admission a spiral staircase. The wheel does not close back to its own "lower" beginning but advances to a "higher" plane. The very terms *lower* and *higher* also show the essential metaphorical nature of thought (see Chapter Eight).

There is also operating at the same time in Wilber's theory a reverse kind of hierarchy than that found in the positivists. Where the positivists put the mathematical and physical sciences first in their pecking order of things, Wilber puts Spirit (ultimate knowledge of the Whole, the Universe) and mind (psychology) before them. While he recognizes that physical nature (body) is certainly necessary for humanity's development in that it emerged out of it (body), psychology, especially transpersonal psychology, is the preeminent vehicle for humanity's knowing its essential nature (Spirit). In Wilber's favorite language, the mind does not *come from* the lower stages but *passes through it* on the way to higher stages. Again we are in the realm of religion, unconventional religion to be sure, as much as we are in psychology. Indeed at this level, there is little if any distinction between them. The farthest reaches of the human psyche lead to the most radical blending of the methods we have evolved for studying the psyche. The methods for knowing the ultimate development of humanity cannot be separated from that development, that is, stage of consciousness. Both reflect one another.

Conclusion: Postscript on Method

The fundamental struggle of the social sciences has been from their very beginning unfold: (1) identifying the basic entities that underlie social life and (2) formulating a set of methods appropriate for studying those entities. This book has argued that stakeholders are the fundamental entities of social life and that assumptions are the basic properties of them. In addition, at the institutional and sociological levels of analysis, I argued that two dimensions in particular, the degree of importance and the degree of certainty, are especially relevant in the ratings of assumptions. I further argued that complex problems demand at the very least a dialectical method of attack. We must have the opportunity of witnessing explicitly at least two different views of a problem, that is, at least two different displays of stakeholder assumptions rated according to their relative importance and certainty.

This basic notion of methodology applies no less to the level of egoic and archetypal stakeholders. The only difference is that at these levels of social analysis the rating dimensions "degree of importance" and "degree of certainty" regarding stakeholder properties (assumptions) are replaced by the more general rating dimensions "degree of potency" and "degree of awareness." These dimensions reflect the fact that at the egoic and archetypal levels of analysis we are concerned with the degree of force or potency that an unconscious, that is, unrecognized, stakeholder exerts over consciousness and the degree of awareness, if not control, that the psyche has over the deeper determinants of itself. The fact that it is exceedingly easy to cross over and pass back and forth between these two sets of dimensions, not to mention very different kinds of stakeholders, shows exactly why social analysis is so difficult to perform. In a word, the psyche neither exists nor can be understood independent of the psychosocial system in which it is a part.

If we follow the implications of Wilber's ideas further, the picture is even more complicated. In an interview with Wilber in the journal *Re Vision* (1981a), Wilber presented a considerably less complicated version of his ideas. What he did was array the terms *Spirit, Mind,* and *Matter* in a column. Matter is placed on the bottom, Mind in the middle, and Spirit, naturally, on top. This columnar array is supposed to represent the ascending development of humanity's nature and of the different types of knowledge appropriate to each higher stage of development. At this point, Wilber introduces a parallel column of the same three levels, Matter, Mind, and Spirit. Next, he draws certain connecting lines between the two columns.

Figure 13, an approximation of Wilbur's conceptual arrangement, illustrates that, as there are different modes of

Figure 13. Modes of Being and of Knowing.

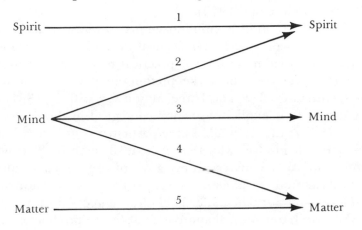

Being, that is, existence or development in a person's psyche, there are also different modes for knowing each level. Level 5, for instance, is what Wilber correctly identifies as pure physical sensory knowing, that is, the body knows itself only as body through its own sensory apparatus. Mind knowing itself as mind, level 3, he labels mental, and Spirit knowing itself as Spirit, or level 1, he labels, not too surprisingly, Spiritual. What is interesting and significant is that Wilber correctly sees that level 3 knowing can be expanded into two other subsets or types, 2 and 4. Level 2 is where mind attempts to know or to understand Spirit and level 4 is where mind attempts to know matter. Following Habermas, Wilber notes that when the mind attempts to know or to have sensory knowledge, its method is empirical-analytic and its interest is called technical. While this may be appropriate for mind knowing matter, it is not appropriate for mind knowing other minds or stakeholders as human, purposeful entities. Unfortunately, this is still the primary mode of knowing in the social and organizational sciences. It is overwhelming that most studies of organizations are of this kind. They attempt to reduce mindful entities and processes to physical ones; hence they attempt to collect physical measures of mindful processes. As a result, they fundamentally distort the nature of the reality that is characteristic of purposeful behavior in organizations. A rare and therefore welcome exception is that of Burrell and Morgan (1979).

When the mind as mind attempts to know other minds, the method is called hermenentic, historical, or phenomenological; its corresponding interest is practical or moral. This is precisely the level for which the methodology of assumptional analysis (Chapters Two and Three; Mason and Mitroff, 1981) was formulated. It is explicitly phenomenological in the senses described earlier; that is, it allows the participants in a situation to witness for themselves why they view it differently. The method of assumptional analysis is my attempt to found a genuinely practical method for phenomenological analysis, and not to do as all too many do: talk endlessly about the necessity for founding a practical, operational approach but fail to provide one precisely because they get hung up in endless discussions about what a "true method" of phenomenological analysis would look like. This is truly Chiliast (that is, dreamer) inquiry at its worst.

The last form, level 2, is one that Habermas does not cover but, as I have indicated, is one that is of fundamental interest to Wilber. Its mode is paradoxical or radically dialectical. Its interest is soteriological, that is, spiritual enlightenment or salvation. It is precisely at this point that the methods of knowing that we in the West have called science and the interests behind them diverge the most from what we have called religion. Yet the merging of these two, science and religion, or at the very least the breaking down of the sharpness of the barriers between them, is the implication that seems to follow from the work of the eleven thinkers who have been our major guides in this book.

In the end, can we continue to deny any longer that there is a fundamental religious aspect to all organizations—that in their attempt to give purpose and meaning to peoples' lives, to fill up their time, that religious instincts are there no matter how disguised they might be? Measured against this notion, how impoverished our concepts and our methods of studying organizations have been.

Every age has the kind of hero or heroine archetype that is appropriate to it. The quest for the Newtons and the Einsteins, for example, of social science is a quest for the heroes that are appropriate for an earlier age and for a different kind of science. The heroes and heroines I seek are those who are appropriate for the study of the mind conceived of as a spiritual entity. The goal of the quest is to allow the psyche of humanity to develop to its highest aesthetic, ethical, and religious ideals.

If the view of social science outlined here makes any sense at all, then it means that the social sciences' search for their Newton has been seriously—dangerously—misguided (Sarason, 1981). Newton is an appropriate character for unification in the mechanical sense only. However, in the teleological sense of unification, the figure of Adam may be a more fitting character, for Adam is at least one character that comes closest to representing the symbol of unification sought after in this discussion. In this condition all archetypes are no longer merely contained in one another, but they are developed to their highest level of potency and mutual support. Their true nature is also recognized as such for what they are. They are not denied by any aspect of the psyche. They are, in short, assimilated by one another. Adam is indeed a fitting character for this state: 'Adam stands not only for the psyche, but for its totality; he is a symbol of the self, and hence a visualization of the 'irrepresentable" Godhead" (Jung, 1963, p. 390).

If this is so, then we await the coming of our Adams or Eves of social science. The ushering in of a new era in social science is thus, in part, equivalent to the creation of a new guiding character. To play on a saying of Freud's, where once Newton was, Adam shall be. May we learn how to develop the kind of science that knows how to nourish and to cherish the Adams and Eves potentially in all of us.

CHAPTER TEN

Summary of Implications for Understanding Organizations

The theory of mind, organizations, and society presented in this book is intricate; as a result, it is of necessity long. Here we summarize some of its key features in the hope that the reader will develop a "feel" for the overall spirit of the theory. Further, since the "theory" presented is more of a programmatic call-to-action, that is, an agenda for future work rather than a completed edifice, it is hoped that the summary will help orient the reader to the never-ending and constantly evolving work that needs to be done.

The summary is presented in the form of a series of key propositions or statements, each of which is elaborated briefly.

1. *The growing complexity of the world has rendered increasingly suspect, if not obsolete, our old pictures of the world.* By a "picture of the world" I mean an underlying base conception or taken-for-granted image of the nature of the social world, that is, what the basic stuff or fundamental parts of society are and how they fit together to constitute an interconnected whole.

The old picture of society was based on a number of underlying assumptions. They are more suspect than ever before. These assumptions were embodied in the form of a number of sharp distinctions. Thus, for instance, there was supposedly a sharp distinction between what goes on (1) inside and underneath the skin of individuals and (2) outside of them in the external environment. As a result, there was also a clear demarcation between scientific disciplines. Thus psychology, for the most part, studied the surface features of the minds of individuals. In a few cases, psychology even penetrated a few steps below the surface to give a deeper account of the mind inside the individual. Economics, political science, and sociology, however, supposedly studied the interactions between collectivities or groups of individuals in the mass, that is, external to individuals.

In the newly evolving picture of the world, what Ackoff (1981) and others such as Churchman (1979) have called the systems approach, all of these distinctions either collapse or become irrelevant, if not dangerous, to our ability to make sense of and to cope with an increasingly complex world. *Where the inside of the mind of the individual leaves off and where the outside of the forces of society supposedly starts or takes over is increasingly blurred.* The theory of mind outlined in this book postulates that neither the behavior of individuals (the "inside") nor of institutions (the "outside") can be understood independently of one another.

2. *The old picture of the world implicitly assumed that the behavior of institutions and organizations could be understood in terms of a relatively small and limited number of internal and external stakeholder forces.* For the most part, these stakeholders were primarily the stockholders, the upper executive levels of the organization and the clients in the external environment. By contrast, in the newly evolving picture of the world, the modern public and private organization is buffeted increasingly by a larger, continually shifting, and, at times, bewildering array of stakeholder forces. There seems to be no end to the number of stakeholders, internal or external, that the modern institution must deal with. Thus, for instance, every organization must monitor seriously the shifting behavior, beliefs, aspirations, and so forth, of such groups as its hourly employees, sales force, professional staff, suppliers, competition, governmental regulatory agencies, to mention only a few. As the re-

cent environment demonstrates time and again, the failure to consider seriously the broadest possible array of stakeholder forces, and especially their changing beliefs, tastes, and so on, can spell disaster for all too many organizations. A poignant and perhaps typical example is the recent plight of the American automobile companies who did not take seriously the threat of Japanese competition and the shifting tastes of the American car-buying public before it was almost too late.

3. *In the old picture of the world the behavior of a relatively limited number of stakeholders could be confined to or understood primarily in terms of economic properties.* The old picture of the world was founded primarily on the metaphor of a machine (Ackoff, 1981). By definition, a machine is something that can be decomposed into its separate parts or components. Also by definition, a machine is something that can be objectified. That is, it has no emotions or feelings. Thus, its workings can be described in purely impersonal terms. Hence, economics, among many, was and still is a natural language in which to describe the workings of a society or an organization conceived of as a machine. The behavior of and between individuals also could supposedly be described as a series of impersonal economic transactions.

By contrast, in the newly evolving picture of the world, the behavior of separate individuals and between groups of individuals is much more complex. Economic transactions, while absolutely indispensable to our understanding of human behavior (Diesing, 1962), describe at best only a limited set of human actions. Modern psychology, systematically conceived, postulates that in addition to economic forces, humanity is driven by innumerable forces of which it is only dimly aware.

This implies that there is at least a double line of potential influence between any two stakeholders in a complex social system. For example, one line of influence concerns economic transactions. In return for needed goods and services supplied by a producing organization, the clients or customers return economic revenue to the organization. This line of mutual influence or dependency, however important, does not exhaust the full range of potential interactions between stakeholders, in this case, producer and client.

It is in the nature of human nature that whenever any two human beings, groups, institutions, or even societies interact or have a vested interest in one another, they develop a psychological portrait of one another. It is in the nature of human nature to form idealized images—both positive and negative—of one another, to project desired and undesired aspects of one's self onto others, to form potentially strong emotional bonds with each other, and, in some cases, to identify so strongly with others that one actually—unconsciously, of course—takes aspects of another's personality into one's own. If all human beings could do is deal with one another in impersonal ways, then we would truly be inhuman. We would then, indeed, be like machines—no emotion, no feeling, no warmth, and ultimately nothing.

4. *Examination of the deepest layers of the human psyche reveals that there is a very special set of stakeholders, known as archetypes, which has been almost totally ignored in modern theories of organization but which nonetheless exerts a considerable hold on the behavior of individuals, groups, organizations, and even whole societies.* In a word, if the composition of the external social world can be fruitfully thought of as an organized collection of diverse stakeholder groups, organizations, and institutions, then the composition of the internal psyche of the individual can also be thought of as an organized collection of diverse internal stakeholders. The set of stakeholders that make up the deepest layers of the mind are known as archetypes. Archetypes are, in brief, the most potent and purest set of symbolic images that the human mind is capable of forming about any entity in its environment that it comes in contact with. Some examples are the Good Mother, the Bad or Evil Mother (the Witch), and the Absolutely Perfect Circle (indicating psychological wholeness or completeness).

Archetypes can be shown to obey a very different set of properties or "laws" than do stakeholders at the macro or external level of society. An analogy with physics may be helpful here. Entities such as electrons and protons at the subatomic level obey a different set of physical laws than do entities at the macro level of everyday life. It is no different with psychological entities.

To date, social scientists have studied only a very limited set of interactions across levels and types of stakeholders at either the macro, external, level of society or the micro, internal, level of the psyche of the individual. To a large extent, this is due to the extreme and, I would argue, dysfunctional disciplinary organization of the modern university. To another extent, it is due to the extreme difficulty in attempting to account for the sources of influence on human behavior across radically different levels of existence. As I have argued throughout this book, we now have no viable alternative but to study the interactions between the forces governing human behavior, no matter from which level they emanate. One only has to look at modern contemporary society to see powerful archetypal forces and imagery breaking out everywhere. Fear now haunts all of us in our everyday lives. More and more nations as well as individuals seem unable to break out of the patterns of mutual distrust and fear that they have learned to project onto one another for so long. Whenever stereotypes abound, one can be sure that archetypal imagery is lurking not far beneath the surface.

5. *Not only are our old pictures of the world outworn and increasingly less capable of dealing with the complexities of modern life but so are the methods of treating problems that were founded on the old pictures.* The old methods were largely founded on a mechanistic conception of the world. Hence, they strove for completeness, closure, and certainty before action was warranted. In contrast, newer methods for attacking complex problems are being developed that realize that if completeness, closure, and certainty were required before action was warranted, then action would never be warranted (Mason and Mitroff, 1981). One would have to wait forever.

Assumptions form the crux of modern life. There is nothing more critical that the managers of all organizations, large and small, public and private, can do than to examine the assumptions that they make about themselves and their environment (Mason and Mitroff, 1981). Nothing is certain anymore or stable forever. A study of the forces that make it necessary to examine more and more assumptions and an outline of a method for accomplishing this critical task have been the guiding aims of this book.

References

Ackoff, R. L. *Creating the Corporate Future: Plan or Be Planned For.* New York: Wiley, 1981.

Ackoff, R. L., and Emery, F. *On Purposeful Systems.* Chicago: Aldine-Atherton, 1974.

Adams, R. R. "Come Cast a Spell with Me." *Softline,* 1982, *1* (4), 30–36.

Allison, G. T. *Essence of Decision: Explaining the Cuban Missile Crisis.* Boston: Little, Brown, 1971.

Anderson, C. M. "Self-Image Therapy." In R. J. Corsini (Ed.), *Handbook of Innovative Psychotherapies.* New York: Wiley, 1981.

Bates, F. L., and Harvey, C. C. *The Structure of Social Systems.* New York: Gardner, 1975.

Bennis, W. G. "Defenses Against 'Depressive Anxiety' in Groups: The Case of the Absent Leader." *Merrill-Palmer Quarterly of Behavior and Development,* 1961, *7,* 1–30.

Berg, P. O. "Emotional Structures in Organizations: A Study of the Process of Change in a Swedish Company." Ph.D. Dissertation. Lund, Sweden: University of Lund, 1979.

Berne, E. *Games People Play: The Psychology of Human Relationship.* New York: Grove, 1964.

Berne, E. *The Structure and Dynamics of Organizations.* New York: Grove, 1966.

Bettelheim, B. *The Uses of Enchantment: The Meaning and Importance of Fairy Tales.* New York: Vintage, 1977.

Bettelheim, B. "Freud and the Soul." *The New Yorker,* March 1, 1982, pp. 52–93.

Bion, W. R. *Experience in Groups.* London: Tavistock, 1959.

Bramson, R. *Coping with Difficult People.* New York: Anchor, 1981.

Broms, H., and Gahmberg, H. "Mythology in Management Decisions." Finland: Helsinki School of Economics, 1980.

Brown, N. *Life Against Death, The Psychoanalytical Meaning of History.* New York: Vintage, 1959.

Burrell, G., and Morgan, G. *Sociological Paradigms and Organizational Analysis.* London: Heinemann, 1979.

Campbell, J. *The Flight of the Wild Gander, Explorations in the Mythological Dimension.* South Bend, Ind.: Regnery/Gateway, 1979.

Carroll, J. "In Spite of Intellectuals." *Theory and Society,* 1978, *6,* 133–150.

Chubin, D. "The Conceptualization of Scientific Specialities." *Sociological Quarterly,* 1976, *17,* 448–476.

Churchman, C. W. *Prediction and Optimal Decision: Philosophical Issues of a Source of Values.* Englewood Cliffs, N.J.: Prentice-Hall, 1961.

Churchman, C. W. *The Design of Inquiring Systems.* New York: Basic Books, 1971.

Churchman, C. W. *The Systems Approach and Its Enemies.* New York: Basic Books, 1979.

Corsini, R. (Ed.). *Current Psychotherapies.* Itasca, Ill.: Peacock, 1979.

Corsini, R. (Ed.). *Handbook of Innovative Psychotherapies.* New York: Wiley-Interscience, 1981.

Deal, T., and Kennedy, A. A. "Who Has the Power in the Corporate Clan?" *Savy,* June, 1982, pp. 40–44.

Deal, T., and Kennedy, A. A. *Corporate Cultures: The Rites and Rituals of Corporate Life.* Reading, Mass.: Addison-Wesley, 1982a.

de Board, R. *The Psychoanalysis of Organizations.* London: Tavistock, 1978.

de Vries, M., and Kets, F. R. *Organizational Paradoxes.* London: Tavistock, 1980.

Dewey, J. *The Quest for Certainty.* New York: Macmillan, 1929.

Diesing, P. *Reason in Society, Five Types of Decisions and Their Social Conditions.* Champaign: University of Illinois, 1962.

Dusay, J., and Dusay, K. M. "Transactional Analysis." In R. J. Corsini (Ed.), *Current Psychotherapies.* Itasca, Ill.: Peacock, 1979.

Feyerabend, P. *Science in a Free Society.* London: NLB, 1978.

Frye, N. *Anatomy of Criticism.* Princeton, N.J.: Princeton University Press, 1973.

Gentry, D. L. "Brief Therapy I." In R. J. Corsini (Ed.), *Handbook of Innovative Psychotherapies.* New York: Wiley, 1981.

George, A. L. *Presidential Decision Making in Foreign Policy: The Effective Use of Information and Advice.* Boulder, Colo.: Westview, 1981.

Gibbard, G., Hartman, J., and Mann, R. (Eds.). *Analysis of Groups: Contributions to Theory, Research, and Practice.* San Francisco: Jossey-Bass, 1978.

Giddens, A. *Central Problems in Social Theory, Action, Structure, and Contradiction in Social Analysis.* Berkeley: University of California Press, 1979.

Girard, R. *Violence and the Sacred.* Baltimore, Md.: Johns Hopkins University Press, 1977.

Harding, M. E. *The I and the Not-I, A Study in the Development of Consciousness.* Princeton, N.J.: Princeton University Press, 1965.

Harrison, R., and Lubin, B. "Personal Style, Group Composition, and Learning." In N. Smelser and W. Smelser (Eds.), *Personality and Social Systems.* New York: Wiley, 1970, pp. 572-581.

Hellriegel, D., and Slocum, J. "Managerial Problem-Solving Styles." *Business Horizons,* 1975, *18,* 29-37.

Hellriegel, D., and Slocum, J. "Preferred Organizational Designs and Problem-Solving Styles: Interesting Companions." *Human Systems Management,* 1980, *1,* 151-158.

Hillman, J. *The Myth of Analysis.* Evanston, Ill.: Northwestern, 1972.

Hillman, J. *Revisioning Psychology*. New York: Harper & Row, 1975a.

Hillman, J. "The Fiction of Case History: A Round." In J. B. Wiggins (Ed.), *Religion as Story*. New York: Harper & Row, 1975b. (Republished in *Healing Fiction* by James Hillman, Barrytown, N.Y.: Station Hill Press, 1983. Excerpts reprinted by permission.)

Hillman, J. *Loose Ends: Primary Papers in Archetypal Psychology*. Irving, Tex.: Spring Publications, 1978.

Hirsch, P. "Ambushes, Shootouts, and Knights of the Round Table: The Language of Corporate Takeovers." In P. Frost, G. Morgan, and L. Pondy (Eds.), *Organizational Symbolism*. Greenwich, Conn.: JAI Press, forthcoming.

Jacobi, J. *Complex/Archetype/Symbol in the Psychology of C. G. Jung*. (R. Manheim, Trans.) Bollingen Series 57. Princeton, N.J.: Princeton University Press, 1959.

James, W. "On Some Mental Effects of the Earthquake." In *Memories and Studies*. London: Longmans Green, 1911.

Jaynes, J. *The Origin of Consciousness in the Breakdown of the Bicameral Mind*. Boston: Houghton Mifflin, 1976.

Jung, C. G. *Psychological Types*. London: Routledge and Kegan Paul, 1923.

Jung, C. G. *Mysterium Coniunctionis: An Inquiry into the Separation and Synthesis of Psychic Opposites in Alchemy*. Princeton, N.J.: Princeton University Press, 1963.

Jung, C. G. *Analytical Psychology*. New York: Vintage, 1968.

Jung, C. G. *Four Archetypes, Mother/Rebirth/Spirit/Trickster*. Princeton, N.J.: Princeton University Press, 1973.

Kadis, A. L., and others. *Practicum of Group Psychotherapy*. New York: Harper & Row, 1974.

Klein, M. *Lives People Live: A Textbook of Transactional Analysis*. New York: Wiley, 1980.

Kuhn, A. *The Logic of Social Systems: A Unified, Deductive, System-Based Approach to Social Science*. San Francisco: Jossey-Bass, 1974.

Lakoff, G., and Johnson, M. *Metaphors We Live By*. Chicago: University of Chicago Press, 1980.

Leach, E. *Culture and Communication*. Cambridge: Cambridge University Press, 1976.

Loevinger, J. *Ego Development: Conceptions and Theories.* San Francisco: Jossey-Bass, 1980.

Maccoby, M. *The Gamesman.* New York: Bantam, 1976.

McCully, R. *Rorschach Theory and Symbolism, A Jungian Approach to Clinical Material.* Baltimore, Md.: Williams & Wilkins, 1971.

Martin, J., Feldman, M., Hatch, M., and Sitkin, S. "The Uniqueness Paradox in Organizational Stories." Working Paper, Graduate School of Business, Stanford University, Palo Alto, California, August, 1982.

Mason, R., and Mitroff, I. *Challenging Strategic Planning Assumptions.* New York: Wiley, 1981.

Miles, R., Snow, C., Meyer, A., and Coleman, H. "Organizational Structure, Strategy, and Process." *Academy of Management Review,* 1978, *3,* 1–17.

Milich, M. "The Wonderful Wizard of Ogdensburg: Robert Woodhead." *Softline,* 1982, *1* (4), 38–41.

Mitroff, I. *The Subjective Side of Science.* Amsterdam: Elsevier, 1974.

Mitroff, I. "Is a Periodic Table of the Elements for Organization Behaviour Possible? Integrating Jung and TA for Organizational Analysis." *Human Systems Management,* 1981, *2,* 168–176.

Mitroff, I., and Kilmann, R. "Stories Managers Tell: A New Tool for Organizational Problem Solving." *Management Review,* July 1975, pp. 18–28.

Mitroff, I., and Kilmann, R. "On Organizational Stories: An Approach to the Design and Analysis of Organizations Through Myths and Stories." In R. H. Kilmann, L. R. Pondy, and D. P. Slevin (Eds.), *The Management of Organization Design.* Dordrecht, Holland: North Holland, 1976.

Mitroff, I., and Kilmann, R. *Methodological Approaches to Social Science: Integrating Divergent Concepts and Theories.* San Francisco: Jossey-Bass, 1978.

Mitroff, I., and Mason, R. "Structuring Ill-Structured Policy Issues: Further Explorations in a Methodology for Messy Problems." *Strategic Management Journal,* 1980, *1,* 331–342.

Mitroff, I., and Mason, R. *Creating a Dialectical Social Science.* Amsterdam: Reidel, 1981a.

Mitroff, I., and Mason, R. "Dialectical Pragmatism: A Progress Report on an Interdisciplinary Program of Research on the Dialectical Inquiry System." *Synthese,* 1981b.

Mitroff, I. I., Mason, R., and Barabba, V. "Policy as Argument: A Logic for Ill-Structured Decision Problems." *Management Science,* 1983a, *28,* 1391–1404.

Mitroff, I., Mason, R., and Barabba, V. *The 1980 Census: Policy-Making Amid Turbulence.* Lexington, Mass.: Lexington, 1983b.

Mitroff, I., and Mitroff, D. "Interpersonal Communication for Knowledge Utilization: Putting Freud and Jung Back Together Again!" *Knowledge,* 1979, *1,* 203–218.

Mitroff, I., and Mitroff, D. "Personality and Problem Solving: Making the Link Visible." *Journal of Experiential Learning and Simulation,* 1980, *2,* 111–119.

Murray, H. A. (Ed.). *Myth and Mythmaking.* Boston: Beacon Press, 1968.

Myers, I. B., and Briggs, K. C. *Myers-Briggs Type Indicator.* Princeton, N.J.: Educational Testing Service, 1962.

Neumann, E. *The Great Mother, An Analysis of the Archetype.* Princeton, N.J.: Princeton University Press, 1955.

Neumann, E. *The Origins and History of Consciousness.* (R. F. C. Hull, Trans.) Bollingen Series 42. Princeton, N.J.: Princeton University Press, 1970.

Nichols, S. *Jung and Tarot, An Archetypal Journey.* New York: Samuel Weiser, 1980. (Portions reprinted by permission of Samuel Weiser, Inc., York Beach, Maine 03910.)

Novak, M. " 'Story' and Experience." In J. B. Wiggins (Ed.), *Religion as Story.* New York: Harper & Row, 1975.

Ogilvy, J. *Many Dimensional Man.* New York: Harper & Row, 1977.

Ouspensky, P. D. *In Search of the Miraculous.* New York: Harvest, 1977.

Parsons, T. "Social Structure and the Development of Personality: Freud's Contribution to the Integration of Psychology and Sociology." In N. Smelser and W. Smelser (Eds.), *Personality and Social Systems.* New York: Wiley, 1970, pp. 48–69.

Parsons, T., and Shils, E. (Eds.). *Toward a General Theory of Action.* Cambridge: Harvard University Press, 1951.

Popper, K. R. *Objective Knowledge: An Evolutionary Approach.* Oxford, England: Clarendon Press, 1972.

Porter, M. *Competitive Strategy.* New York: Free Press, 1980.

Price, D. J. de S. *Little Science, Big Science.* New York: Columbia University Press, 1963.

Propp, V. *Morphology of the Folktale.* Austin: University of Texas, 1968.

Roheim, G. *Psychoanalysis and Anthropology, Culture, Personality, and the Unconscious.* New York: International Universities Press, 1950.

Sarason, S. B. *Psychology Misdirected.* New York: Free Press, 1981.

Secord, P. (Ed.). *Explaining Human Behavior.* Beverly Hills, Calif.: Sage, 1982.

Sheikh, A. A., and Jordan, C. S. "Eidetic Psychotherapy." In R. J. Corsini (Ed.), *Handbook of Innovative Psychotherapies.* New York: Wiley, 1981.

Singer, E. A. *Experience and Reflection.* Philadelphia: University of Pennsylvania Press, 1959.

Slater, P. *Microcosm, Structural, Psychological, and Religious Evolution in Groups.* New York: Wiley, 1966.

Slater, P. E. *The Glory of Hera, Greek Mythology and the Greek Family.* Boston: Beacon Press, 1968.

Slater, P. "On Social Regression." In N. Smelser and W. Smelser (Eds.), *Personality and Social Systems.* New York: Wiley, 1970, pp. 70-99.

Slocum, J. "Does Cognitive Style Affect Diagnosis and Intervention Strategies of Change Agents?" *Group and Organizational Studies,* 1978, *3,* 199-210.

Smelser, N. J., and Smelser, W. T. (Eds.). *Personality and Social Systems.* New York: Wiley, 1970.

Steckroth, R. L., Slocum, J. W., and Sims, H. P. "Organizational Roles, Cognitive Roles, and Problem Solving Styles." *Journal of Experiential Learning and Simulation,* 1980, *2,* 77-87.

Stevens, A. *Archetypes.* New York: William Morrow, 1982.

Swanson, G. *The Birth of the Gods, The Origin of Primitive Beliefs.* Ann Arbor: University of Michigan Press, 1974.

Swatez, G. M. "Social Organization of a University Laboratory."

Unpublished Ph.D. dissertation, University of California, Berkeley, 1966.

Thompson, J. *Organizations in Action*. New York: McGraw-Hill, 1967.

Thompson, W. *At the Edge of History*. New York: Harper & Row, 1971.

Toffler, A. *The Third Wave*. New York: William Morrow, 1980.

Tomkins, S. S. "Script Theory: Differential Magnification of Affects." In H. E. Howe (Ed.), *Nebraska Symposium on Motivation, 1978*. Lincoln: University of Nebraska Press, 1979.

Toulmin, S. *The Uses of Argument*. Cambridge: Cambridge University Press, 1958.

Toulmin, S., Rieke, R., and Janik, A. *An Introduction to Reasoning*. New York: Macmillan, 1979.

Turner, V. *Dramas, Fields, and Metaphors, Symbolic Action in Human Society*. Ithaca, N.Y.: Cornell University Press, 1974.

von Franz, M. L. *Creation Myths*. Zurich: Spring, 1972.

von Franz, M. L. *Projection and Re-Collection in Jungian Psychology*. London: Open Court, 1978.

von Franz, M. L. *Shadow and Evil in Fairy Tales*. Irving, Texas: Spring, 1980.

von Franz, M. L. *Puer Aeternus*. Santa Monica, Calif.: Sigo, 1981.

von Franz, M. *Interpretation of Fairy Tales*. Dallas, Texas: Spring, 1982.

Watkins, J. G., and Watkins, H. H. "Ego-State Therapy." In R. J. Corsini (Ed.), *Handbook of Innovative Psychotherapies*. New York: Wiley, 1981.

Wickes, F. *The Inner World of Childhood*. Englewood Cliffs, N.J.: Spectrum, 1966.

Wilber, K. *The Spectrum of Consciousness*. London: Theosophical, 1977.

Wilber, K. *The Atman Project*. London: Theosophical, 1980.

Wilber, K. "Reflections on the New-Age Paradigm." *ReVision*, Spring, 1981a, 53–74.

Wilber, K. *Up From Eden, A Transpersonal View of Human Evolution*. New York: Anchor, 1981b.

Wrong, D. "The Oversocialized Conception of Man in Modern Sociology." In N. Smelser and W. Smelser (Eds.), *Personality and Social Systems*. New York: Wiley, 1970, pp. 113–124.

Index

173